SPACE GALAXY & FRONTIERS

SANDEEP BISHT

Made with ♥ on the Notion Press Platform
www.notionpress.com

To the dreamers who refuse to believe that the sky is the limit.

To every scientist, engineer, astronaut, explorer, student, and curious mind who looks at the night sky and sees not distant stars, but endless possibilities.

This book is dedicated to those who dare to ask questions that have no easy answers, who challenge the boundaries of human knowledge, and who believe that every great discovery begins with curiosity. I dedicate this work to my parents and family, whose unwavering support gave me the courage to pursue knowledge, and to my teachers and mentors, who taught me that learning is the first step toward innovation.

Above all, I dedicate this book to humanity. May future generations continue to explore the galaxies beyond our reach, protect our home planet, and build a civilization where science, wisdom, and compassion guide our journey among the stars.

As we stand on the frontier of a new space age, may this book inspire readers to dream boldly, think critically, and never stop exploring the magnificent universe that surrounds us.

The universe is vast, but human curiosity is boundless.

— Sandeep Bisht

Contents

Foreword

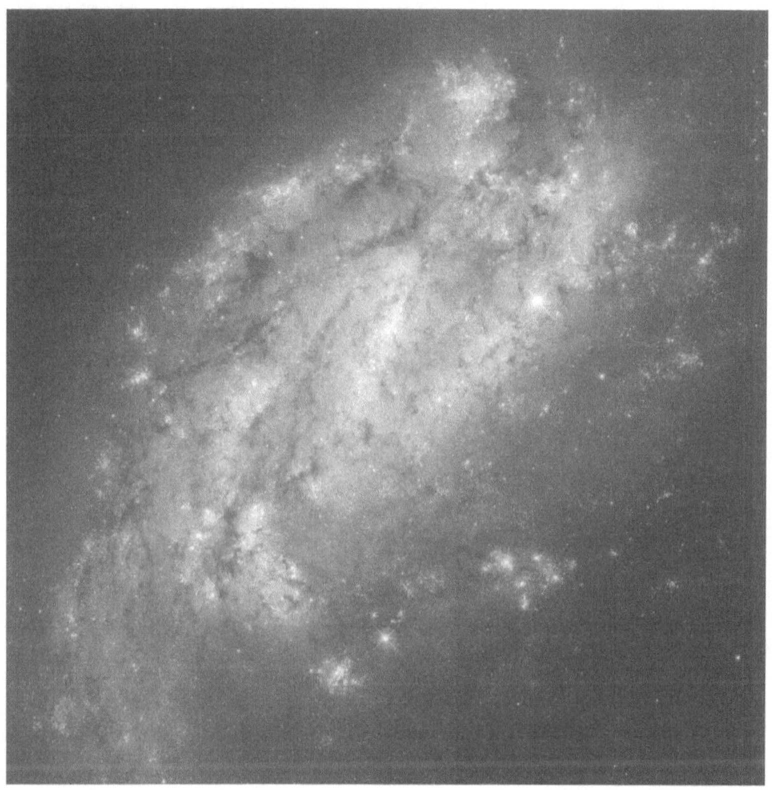

Humanity has always been fascinated by the stars. From ancient civilizations mapping constellations to modern observatories peering billions of light-years into the cosmos, our desire to understand the universe has remained constant. Every generation has expanded the boundaries of knowledge, revealing that the universe is far more vast, mysterious, and interconnected than we once imagined.

Space Galaxy & Frontier invites readers on a journey through this extraordinary cosmic landscape. It explores the structure of galaxies, the evolution of stars, the formation of planets, the nature of black holes, the search for extraterrestrial life, and the technological advances that are opening new frontiers in space exploration. While some topics remain active areas of scientific research, the book distinguishes established scientific understanding from ongoing questions and emerging ideas.

This book is written for students, science enthusiasts, educators, researchers, and anyone inspired by the wonders of the universe. Complex scientific concepts are presented in an accessible manner, encouraging readers to develop both curiosity and critical thinking. Rather than simply presenting facts, the book aims to inspire readers to ask deeper questions about our place in the cosmos and the future of human exploration.

The twenty-first century marks a remarkable era in space science. Powerful telescopes are revealing galaxies formed shortly after the Big Bang. Robotic spacecraft continue to explore our Solar System, while preparations for sustained human missions to the Moon and, eventually, Mars are underway. Private space companies are accelerating innovation, making space more accessible than ever before. Together, these developments are transforming what was once considered science fiction into scientific reality.

Scientific progress has always depended on imagination, evidence, collaboration, and perseverance. Every breakthrough begins with a question, and every discovery opens the door to new mysteries. The universe continues to challenge our understanding, reminding us that there is always more to learn.

May this book inspire you to observe the night sky with renewed wonder, appreciate the remarkable achievements of science, and perhaps contribute to the discoveries that will shape the future of space exploration. The frontier of space is not merely a destination—it is an invitation to explore, innovate, and expand the horizons of human knowledge.

Sandeep Bisht

Preface

Space has fascinated humanity since the beginning of civilization. Every generation has looked toward the stars with wonder, asking fundamental questions: How did the universe begin? What lies beyond our galaxy? Are we alone in the cosmos? These questions have inspired centuries of observation, scientific inquiry, and technological innovation.

Space Galaxy & Frontier was written to provide readers with a comprehensive introduction to the science of the universe while encouraging a lifelong curiosity about space exploration. This book brings together key concepts from astronomy, astrophysics, cosmology, planetary science, and modern space technology in a way that is accessible to students, educators, researchers, and anyone interested in understanding the cosmos.

Throughout these pages, readers will explore the birth and evolution of stars, the structure of galaxies, the mysteries of black holes and dark matter, the search for exoplanets, the possibility of life beyond Earth, and the technologies that are shaping humanity's future in space. Where topics involve active scientific debate or ongoing research, the book distinguishes established evidence from hypotheses and emerging ideas.

Science is constantly evolving. New telescopes, satellites, space probes, and missions continue to expand our understanding of the universe. While every effort has been made to present accurate and up-to-date information at the time of writing, readers are encouraged to continue exploring new discoveries as space science advances.

This book is not intended to replace academic textbooks or scientific journals. Instead, it serves as a bridge between complex scientific research and the curiosity of readers who wish to understand the universe more deeply. My goal is to make space science engaging, thought-provoking, and inspiring without losing scientific accuracy.

I am deeply grateful to my family, teachers, mentors, fellow researchers, and the global scientific community whose dedication has expanded humanity's knowledge of the cosmos. Every space mission, observation, experiment, and scientific publication contributes to our collective understanding of the universe.

Finally, I dedicate this work to every reader who has ever looked at the night sky and wondered what lies beyond the stars. Curiosity has always been the driving force behind discovery, and it is my hope that this book inspires you to keep asking questions, seeking knowledge, and imagining the possibilities that await us beyond our home planet.

The universe is vast, and our journey of discovery has only just begun.

Sandeep Bisht

Acknowledgements

The completion of Space Galaxy & Frontier has been a journey of curiosity, learning, and perseverance. Although this book bears my name, it reflects the contributions and inspiration of many individuals and the broader scientific community.

I express my deepest gratitude to my parents and family for their unwavering encouragement, patience, and belief in my pursuit of knowledge. Their support has been the foundation of every milestone in my journey.

I sincerely thank my teachers, mentors, and educators who nurtured my curiosity and instilled the values of critical thinking, scientific inquiry, and lifelong learning. Their guidance has played a significant role in shaping my understanding of science and the universe.

I am grateful to the countless astronomers, physicists, engineers, mathematicians, astronauts, and researchers whose discoveries and dedication have expanded humanity's understanding of space. Their published research, observations, and scientific achievements continue to inspire people around the world and form the foundation of modern space science.

My appreciation also extends to the engineers, mission planners, and support teams behind space observatories, satellites, robotic probes, and human spaceflight programs. Their work has transformed our understanding of the Solar System, distant galaxies, and the broader universe.

I also thank the editors, reviewers, designers, publishers, and everyone involved in bringing this manuscript to completion. Their professionalism and attention to detail have greatly improved the quality of this book.

Finally, I extend my heartfelt gratitude to the readers. Your curiosity, enthusiasm, and passion for exploring the cosmos are the true reasons this book exists. I hope these pages encourage you to ask bold questions, appreciate the beauty of scientific discovery, and continue exploring the remarkable universe we all share.

May our collective pursuit of knowledge continue to unite humanity and inspire future generations to reach beyond the boundaries of what is known.

With sincere gratitude,

Sandeep Bisht

Prologue

On a clear night, when the lights of our cities fade and the sky reveals its countless stars, we witness only a small glimpse of an unimaginably vast universe. Every point of light tells a story that began millions—or even billions—of years ago. Beyond what the naked eye can see lie billions of galaxies, each containing billions of stars, planets, nebulae, and mysteries that continue to challenge our understanding.

Humanity has always been drawn to the heavens. Ancient civilizations tracked the movements of celestial bodies to navigate oceans, mark the seasons, and understand the passage of time. Over centuries, philosophers, astronomers, and scientists transformed curiosity into observation, observation into theory, and theory into discovery. From the invention of the telescope to the launch of sophisticated space observatories and interplanetary spacecraft, every generation has expanded the boundaries of what we know about the cosmos.

Yet, despite remarkable advances in science and technology, many profound questions remain unanswered. What existed before the observable universe formed? What are dark matter and dark energy? How do supermassive black holes shape galaxies? Are there other worlds capable of supporting life? Could intelligent civilizations exist elsewhere in the universe? These questions remind us that every discovery reveals new mysteries waiting to be explored.

This book is an invitation to join that journey of exploration. It examines the formation and evolution of galaxies, the life cycles of stars, the architecture of our Solar System, the physics that governs the universe, and the technologies that are enabling humanity to explore farther than ever before. Along the way, it distinguishes established scientific knowledge from active areas of research, encouraging readers to appreciate both what we know and what remains uncertain.

The "frontier" in this book's title represents more than the edge of physical space. It symbolizes the frontier of human curiosity, imagination, and innovation. Every new telescope, every spacecraft, every scientific breakthrough, and every question asked by a curious mind pushes that frontier a little farther.

Whether you are a student discovering astronomy for the first time, a science enthusiast eager to deepen your understanding, or a lifelong learner inspired by the wonders of the universe, I hope these pages encourage you to think critically, explore fearlessly, and remain open to the endless possibilities that science reveals.

As you turn the page, you begin a journey across space and time—from our own planet to the farthest galaxies visible through modern telescopes. The universe is not merely a distant place beyond our reach; it is the story of our origins, our present, and perhaps our future.

Welcome to the Space Galaxy & frontier.

— Sandeep Bisht

CHAPTER ONE

Our place in the Universe

In an instant of creation about 14 billion years ago the universe burst forth, creating space where there was no space, and time when there was no time. It was so hot and so dense that not even nucleons, the building blocks of atomic nuclei, had as yet formed. Until about 1/100,000th of a second all that existed was an intense fire and primitive particles called quarks and electrons and all their heavier kin together with their antiparticles; in a sense, these were the elementary particles conceived of by two early Greek philosophers of the fifth century BC, Leucippus and his disciple, Democritus. They evidently believed that an end must come to the reduction of matter into smaller parts, which they called atomos. Indeed, elementary particles that we call quarks have been discovered at last in our own time and all attempts to reduce them further have failed. After that first brief moment, the quarks coalesced into neutrons, protons and other versions of these nucleons, never to be free again. In that inferno the lightest elements — deuterium and helium — were forged from the neutrons and protons during the next few minutes. These two primordial elements make up fully one-quarter of the mass in the universe today. Almost all the remaining mass is in that simplest element — hydrogen — consisting of one proton orbited by one electron. The hydrogen nuclei thatwere formed in the first fraction of a second are the same that pervade the universe now. In the very earliest moments, there must have been a slight lumpiness in an otherwise uniformly expanding universe. As the expansion progressed, gravity acted upon those lumps, attracting surrounding matter — the primordial hydrogen and helium — into great tenuous clouds of chaotically swirling gases and the radiation that was trapped inside them. As the radiation slowly leaked from their surfaces and the clouds cooled, they began to collapse and fragment to form proto-galaxies, some slowly turning in one direction, others in another, so that in sum there was no rotation. As the proto-galaxies collapsed further, conservation of their angular momentum caused them to whirl ever faster, just as an ice skater — who goes into a whirl with arms outstretched and draws them in — whirls faster. As each cloud fragment collapsed, it was flattened like a pancake with a central bulge by the increasingly rapid rotation, like the Andromeda Galaxy shown in Figure. At last a balance was reached between the force of gravity that would cause total collapse, and the centrifugal force of rotation, that would spin matter off into space. Because of instabilities within the thin disks, the clouds fragmented further to form stars, some larger than our Sun, and many more of them smaller. When galaxies were first observed in the first century as faint nebulous objects in the sky it was not known that they were enormous collections of stars (Figure). Al Sufi was an astronomer in the court of the Emir in Persia. He observed the great galaxy, Andromeda, as a faint nebulous patch, which he called "little cloud" in his famous Book of Fixed Stars in 964 A.D. And he described other nebulae, some of which are not galaxies at all, but rather dense clouds of gas and dust in our own galaxy, the Milky Way. The Witch Head Nebula, shown in the preface, is one of many beautiful nebula, some of which have an appearance that reminds us of an animal, or of a mythological figure. Not until the late 1700s did William Herschel speculate that some of the hazy patches that he could see among the stars with his telescope were actually "island universes" like our own galaxy, lying far outside it and containing vast numbers of stars. For his accomplishments, William Herschel was knighted by George III of England. His sister, Caroline, too (Figure) made many important discoveries and was the first woman to be recognized as an astronomer with a salary from the King. By the end of her long life she had reaped numerous honors including the gold medal of the Royal Astronomical Society (England)

The Andromeda Galaxy (M31), was first recorded by the Persian astronomer Al Sufi (903–986 A.D.) living in the court of Emir Adud ad-Daula. He described and depicted it in his Book of Fixed Stars (964 A.D.) and called it the "little cloud." The galaxy is composed of about 400 billion stars. It lies relatively close to our own galaxy, the Milky Way, and is rather similar, having a central bulge and flat disk in the form of spiral arms. Relatively close in this context means 2,900,000 light-years (or equivalently a thousand billion kilometers). The two galaxies are attracting each other and will collide and pass through each other, causing distortion of each. Eventually, they will merge. Two smaller elliptical galaxies M32 and M110 (the two bright spots outside the main galaxy) are in orbit about Andromeda. The myriad foreground stars are in our own galaxy. Credit: George Healy obtained this color image of spiral galaxy M31, the Great Galaxy in Andromeda, together with its smaller elliptical satellite galaxies.

Astronomy, being one of the oldest professions in the world, has a long and glorious history, which this short introduction will by no means give justice. Nevertheless, a short description of where the science of astronomy/astrophysics come from is in its place. Astronomy has played a crucial part in the oldest societies known to man, from the Mayan empires over the greek cradle of democracy to the persian and babylonian ancient people. The breathtaking starry night has by many been thought of as godly and/or holy and has inspired people to observe it, describe it and map it. Up through time the surrounding Universe has not only been amazing and fascinating generations, it has also been a constant cause for disputes. It was long thought that Ptolemy's geocentric second century picture of the Universe, where stars and planets all revolve around the Earth, as illustrated in the two left panels, was the correct model. If you proposed otherwise, you were ridiculed or punished. In the renaissance people slowly started to accept that there might be more to the understanding of the Universe than a scheme with the earth in the center and everything else revolving around it. With scientists like Copernicus, Brahe, Kepler, and Galilei significant steps were taken away from the geocentric world picture towards a heliocentric picture as first described by Copernicus, with the planets moving around the Sun on elliptical orbits as described by Kepler (1609). Brahe actually did not believe the heliocentric picture, but his outstanding naked eye(!) observations led Kepler to his discoveries. The heliocentric picture is portrayed as Copernicus imagined it. Moving from the geocentric to the heliocentric world picture was based on observations of the night sky, both with and without telescopes, and the eager to understand and describe these observations by mathematics. With Newton's Philosophiae naturalis principia mathematica (Newton 1760), where he describes the laws of gravitation and derives Kepler's empirical laws of planetary motion for the first time, astronomy entered a new era. In very much the same way, it is this fascination and urge to describe observations of the Universe by mathematics and physics that drives many astronomers today. Taking part in the observing, detailed theoretical description, and mapping of the magnificent Universe around us is a privilege and what makes this profession so great. With this eager to discover and explore the unknown, we have come a long way since the mayans, the babylonians, the greeks, and the astronomers of the renaissance. Not despite of them, but because of them, we today believe that we understand how it all started, what the foundation of it all is, and how it evolved into what it is today. As Bernard of Chartres (and later Sir Isaac Newton) puts it:

The traditional geocentric picture of the Universe as described by Ptolemy in his second century Almagest (left) and in a 'modern' sixteenth century version (center). Copernicus' heliocentric model was first presented and illustrated in "On the Revolutions of the Celestial Sphere" (1543) as shown in the right panel. This model changed the view of our place in the Universe – we were no longer the center of attention.

The Standard Big Bang Model

People slowly started to acknowledge that the earth was not the center of the solar system, let alone the Milky Way Galaxy or the Universe as a whole, and mathematicians, physicists and astronomers were able to theoretically describe the empirical models that existed of larger and larger portions of the observable Universe. With the Messier catalog (re-published in Messier & Niles 1981) and Herschel's Catalogue of Nebulae (Herschel 1786) in the late eighteenth century and later Dreyer's New General Catalog (Dreyer 1888), it became evident that the sky was filled with objects, that were not 'just' stars. Though it had been speculated by several people that these objects were 'island' Universes similar to our own Milky Way at extreme distances, it was not until the work of Hubble in the early 1920s (less than 100 years ago!), that it was finally shown that they were extragalactic. In 1925 Hubble for the first time used Cepheid's relationship between period and absolute magnitude to show that some of the major known nebulae, i.e., galaxies, were indeed extragalactic (Hubble 1925a,b). In Hubble (1926) he showed that extragalactic objects were spread all over the sky and derived the first empirical relations for these objects. Hubble showed that these extragalactic galaxies were all receding from the Milky Way with a velocity strongly dependent on their distance to us (Hubble 1929). This relationship can be formulated in Hubble's law:

$v = H0 \times d$.

Here H0 is the so-called Hubble constant (at present indicated by 0), v the receding velocity of the galaxy and d the distance to the galaxy. Thirteen years earlier Einstein presented his general theory of relativity (Einstein 1916) generalizing the special relativity theory and Newton's laws of gravitation via his field equations (Einstein 1915) providing a unified theory for the behavior of energy, i.e., mass in the spacetime continuum. In Einstein (1917) this theory was put into a cosmological context, and how to obtain stable solution to the field equations was discussed. Einstein created stable solutions by introducing the cosmological constant, Λ, to keep the Universe (artificially) static. Einstein later regretted having introduced Λ, however, as we will describe below, this cosmological constant became an important part of our present understanding of the Universe in the 1980s (though introduced via different reasoning). De Sitter (de Sitter 1917, 1918) and Friedmann (Friedmann 1922, 1924) later showed that stable solutions to Einstein's field equations did indeed exist for expanding as well as stationary models of the Universe, also without introducing the artificial Λ. Hubble was aware of this work in 1929 and therefore noted that the linear distance-velocity relationship from Equation might be a first approximation to the actual movement and behavior of the extragalactic nebulae. At cosmological distances Hubble's law is indeed model dependent, but the Hubble expansion in Equation is nevertheless a fundamental feature of the local Universe.

Having established both theoretically and observationally in the 1920s that the Universe was expanding, it became obvious that in the very distant past the Universe must have been much denser, than it is today. In fact, with enough time available it would at some point have been considered a physical singularity, i.e., it would have been so dense and hot that all physical models would brake down. This singularity has since the early 1950s been known as the Big Bang. The time needed for the Universe to evolve from this singularity into a Universe with the observed expansion rate is simply obtained by inverting Hubble's law in Equation. This results in an approximate age of the Universe, called the Hubble time

$$t_0 \equiv \frac{1}{H_0} = \frac{d}{v} \sim 13.7 \text{ Gyr} .$$

Up through the 40s and 50s people like Gamow, Dicke, Alpher & Herman speculated that this Big Bang over-density should be observable as a smooth background black-body radiation, and they estimated it to have a temperature of the order 10s of Kelvin. In 1965 the cosmic microwave background (CMB) was serendipitously observed for the first time as a spurious 3.5 K background as presented in Penzias & Wilson (1965) and Dicke et al. (1965). This was the second observational evidence (Hubble's distance-velocity relation in Equation being the first) of the Big Bang model of the Universe. With the Cosmic Background Explorer (COBE; Mather et al. 1990; Smoot et al. 1991; Bennett et al. 1996) and Wilkinson Microwave Anisotropy Probe (WMAP; Hinshaw et al. 2009; Jarosik et al. 2007; Bennett et al. 2003; Jarosik et al. 2011) the CMB has later been observed in amazing detail and has backed up these initial findings. In Figure The CMB maps from the COBE 4 years data (left) and the WMAP 5-years data (right) are shown.

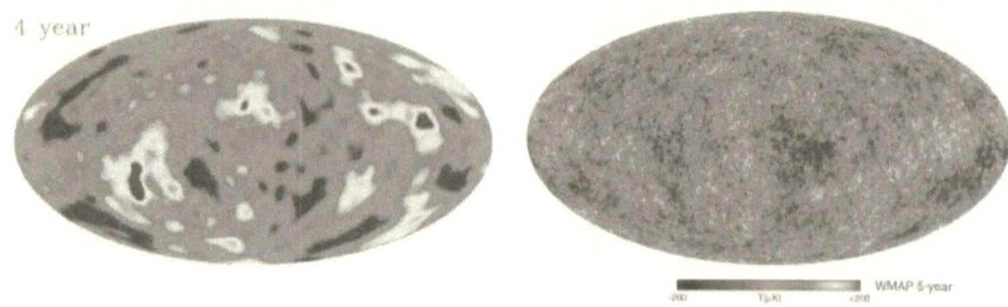

The cosmic microwave background (CMB) from the COBE 4-years data (left; Bennett et al. 1996) and WMAP 5-years data (right; Hinshaw et al. 2009). The color scheme depicts the 13.7 Gyr old temperature (density) fluctuations, which after inflation grew via hierarchical merging and condensation into the galaxies we know and love. This radiation is the left-over from the singularity we call Big Bang and is one of the strongest observational proofs of the standard Big Bang model.

Previously it had been a challenge to explain the high abundance of metals (primarily He) in the local Universe via Hydrogen burning in stars only, so when Hoyle & Tayler (1964) managed to describe the observed He/H ratio within a factor of two, by assuming that the Universe had been a singularity in the past, the road was paved for the general acceptance of the evolutionary Big Bang model.

Structure Formation & (Λ)CDM Building Blocks

Apart from the particle physicists' interest in the formation of the first heavy elements, also a more general theoretical interest in describing the Big Bang model grew in the twentieth century. Many such attempts assumed Einsteins's general relativity to be true. One of the preferred models, in the form of Friedmann's solutions to Einstein's field equations mentioned above, made some strong assumptions. The model assumed that the Universe is isotropic and homogenous. These two main assumptions have come to be known as the cosmological principle. Even though this was just a cosmological restatement of the thoughts behind Corpenicus' heliocentric picture depicted in Figure, i.e., there is nothing special about our location in the Universe, it still seemed odd that this should be the case, now that it was clear that the observable Universe was definitely not isotropic and homogenous. Thus, any theoretical model of how the CMB temperature fluctuations over time turn into the observed galaxies, needed to obey these assumptions if Friedmann's equations were to be right.

Already in Jeans (1902) it was described how a stable structure (in this particular case a spherical nebula) can become unstable and collapse under its own gravity. This happens if the size of the initial density perturbations are larger than the Jeans length

$$\lambda_J = \frac{c_s}{\sqrt{\frac{G\rho_0}{\pi}}},$$

where G is Newton's gravitational constant and cs is the sound speed propagating in the 'medium' of mass density ρ0. This equation simply states that if the spatial (Jeans) scales are large enough the gravitational attraction can overcome the (sound) pressure and collapse. Concerned with only spherically symmetric perturbations Lemaˆıtre (1931, 1933) applied this line of thought to the expanding Universe, assuming the cosmological principle to be true. It was generalized, who studied the evolution of the assumed infinitesimal temperature (density) perturbations in the framework of the Friedmann model. From these different studies the authors however arrived to the conclusion that the observed galaxies could not have formed from gravitational collapse, since the Hubble time, t0 (Equation), was simply too short to allow the assumed infinitesimal perturbations to collapse into structures as massive as galaxies.

In the 1960s various authors allowed the initial density perturbations to be non-infinitesimal, and developed a framework in which structures could collapse, form filaments of over-dense regions (leaving under-dense voids behind), and evolve into the large scale structure of the Universe, which was observed. In the 70s generally two theories came to dominate: the adiabatic and the isothermal model. The adiabatic picture (e.g., Doroshkevich et al. 1974) describes the perturbations as adiabatic sound waves, i.e., sound waves not exchanging energy with the surroundings, which starts to fragment into smaller and smaller structures, as the density contrast of the surroundings changes. Hence, the adiabatic picture is, so to speak, a 'top-down' picture of structure formation, where large structures form first and then fragment into smaller structures. The isothermal picture, on the other hand, is a 'bottom-up' picture, where small structures form first and then merger to grow into larger and larger structures. It describes how isothermal perturbations in balance with the pressure collapse and form larger structures via hierarchical clustering and merging of over-densities. The discovery of the CMB in 1965 served as a direct observational test of the initial conditions of these theories of structure formation. As the CMB measurements improved it became clear that the size of the observed perturbations were simply too small to have been the primordial seeds of baryonic matter, that developed into the massive galaxies observed in the nearby Universe within the age of the Universe, i.e., within t0. The main problem was that the baryons needed to cool significantly before they could collapse (or fragment) due to the counteracting radiation pressure in Jeans' theory. However, along with the development of the theories for baryonic structure formation up through the 70s, the concept of dark matter was discussed extensively as possibly playing a major role in the picture of structure formation – and indeed, dark matter turned out to be the key for solving the t0 time-scale issue.

Dark Matter, predicted already in the early 1930s (Oort 1932; Zwicky 1933), consists of non-baryonic particles neither emitting nor reflecting electromagnetic radiation. It was initially introduced into structure formation as neutrinos with non-zero mass, later referred to as hot dark matter due to the neutrinos' relatively low masses. It was however realized that several other particles, some more exotic than others, but all weakly interacting and much more massive particles (WIMPs) than the neutrinos, could also serve as non-baryonic dark matter1 . In the early 1980s the models for this cold dark matter (CDM)2 were presented. Since dark matter is weakly interacting, or in other words collisionless, the gravitational instability of the CDM perturbations is not hampered by a counteracting radiation pressure. This was the problem baryonic structure formation was facing, and it therefore made the dark matter structure formation picture more attractive.

In Press & Schechter (1974) it had several years earlier been described how the mass function of objects experiencing a hierarchical structure formation, i.e., a bottom-up picture similar to the isothermal structure formation from the same period, under the assumption of an initial gaussian distribution of density perturbations, evolves as a function of time. This theory proved extremely useful for describing the buildup of the CDM hierarchical Universe and was later improved by Lacey & Cole (1993) taking detailed observations of the CMB into account3 . In general, at very early stages the initial gravitational collapse is linear, i.e., the CDM perturbations are slowly collapsing linearly into larger and larger over-densities, which the baryons relentlessly follow. When these overdensities become large enough, the evolution enters a non-linear regime, where the dark matter potential wells collapse to form filaments and voids mapping the CDM 'potential well landscape' that baryons can condense into to form the observable galaxies. In next section we will describe this 'condensation' in a bit more detail. Having established the general picture of structure formation, it was no longer as problematic to state that the Universe was homogeneous and isotropic, i.e., to assume the cosmological principle

1. In principle brown dwarfs, black holes and neutron stars, all baryonic, are also dark matter 'particles' and are usually referred to as MACHOs (massive compact halo objects). However, these were not present in the very early Universe, so here we let the term dark matter refer to the non-baryonic WIMPs only.

2. Also warm dark matter schemes were introduced, but both the hot and warm dark matter models have proven much less successful than the cold dark matter models, and was mostly popular in the late 70s and the 80s. The terms hot, warm and cold refer to the masses of the dark matter particles (CDM being the heaviest), and the epoch at which the particles became relativistic

to hold. Since, if all structures form by the collapse of gaussian perturbations in a large uniform 'fluid' or plasma of particles, it is not hard to imagine that a some characteristic scale the cosmological principle is indeed true. This characteristic scale has been shown by extensive observational efforts the Universe is indeed homogeneous and isotropic and the cosmological principle therefore holds.

Despite the many successes of the standard Big Bang model, there were still unsolved issues that cosmologists in the 1970s were very puzzled by. To obtain the high degree of isotropy that the CMB predicts, the initial conditions of the Big Bang need to be carefully adjusted, fine-tuned, and arranged such that the Universe evolves into what is observed. The five main unsolved issues or problems with the Big Bang model are often referred to as the flatness, horizon, baryon asymmetry, large scale structures and monopole problem.

The flatness problem concerns the fact that the Universe seems to have an energy density very close to the critical density, preventing the geometry of the Universe to be curved, i.e., the Universe is flat. It appears that the Universe was flat to within a factor of ~ 10−16 when it was already 1 second old, which is indeed heavy finetuning.

As mentioned the CMB was observed to be very uniform over the full sky. However, by simply rewinding the clock, every point in the sky could not have been in causal contact and therefore did not have the chance to adjust their temperature in the early Universe if only t0 was available. In other words the horizon of each point in the sky is too small for them to have been in causal contact, so how come the full-sky CMB map is so uniform?

The baryon asymmetry problem deals with the fact that there is an asymmetry between baryons and photons in the Universe today. For this asymmetry to survive the hot early phase of the Big Bang model, there must have been a baryon–anti-baryon asymmetry at early times, which insured that enough baryons were left for the electron-positron pair production.

The large scale structure problem questioned whether there was actually enough time for matter to condense and collapse, as described above, to form the observed large scale structures of the Universe within t0. Lastly, the so-called grand unified theory of particle physics where the electromagnetic, strong, and weak forces were combined in the early Universe, predicts the presence of so-called magnetic monopoles and cosmic strings. Since these have not been observed, their volume density must be approximately 0 at present, which is the essence of the monopole problem. Why are they not here anymore? Thus, all five problems question the initial conditions and consequences of the Big Bang model.

In Guth (1981) and Linde (1982) the inflationary scenario of the early Universe was presented as a solution to these problems. The authors suggested that when the Universe was of the order 10−35 seconds old it went through and exponential inflation.

Through several e-foldings the geometry of the Universe was driven towards flat, the size, i.e., the event horizon was heavily expanded, the baryon-anti-baryon asymmetry was created, the seeds for the large scale structures were 'frozen out', and the density of magnetic monopoles was diluted to almost 0. The inflation therefore solved the five main problems of the Big Bang models.

The inflationary scenario also predicts that the cosmological constant Λ is significantly different from 0, and thereby re-introduces the cosmological constant into Einstein's field equations; though through different reasoning than Einstein's. In the field equations the terms concerning Λ can be thought of as an energy density, and today the astronomical community refers to the cosmological constant contribution as the dark energy of the CDM model. Since the early 1980s inflation has been a crucial part of the modern cosmological picture and the formation history of the Universe, and with the introduction of inflation and dark energy, the CDM model is now referred to as the ΛCDM model.

Despite the extensive observational efforts that supported ΛCDM (CMB, the Hubble expansion, the lack of monopoles and cosmic strings, baryon-photon asymmetry, large scale structures, etc.)4 it wasn't before the late 1990s that the ΛCDM picture was generally accepted. This happened when several authors, using distant supernovae, showed that the expansion of the Universe is indeed accelerating as predicted by the dark energy cosmological constant contribution to the theory. Through these and the CMB efforts, among others, it has been established that the global energy densities of the ΛCDM building blocks, i.e., visible baryonic matter, dark matter and dark energy are remarkably different. It appears that the energy density of the Universe consists of only 4% baryons(!), 23% dark matter and 73% dark energy.

Today ΛCDM with its dark energy component is referred to as the standard model of Big Bang cosmology and structure formation. Hence, today we describe the Universe as having started from a Big Bang (singularity) with perturbations mainly consisting of dark matter, running through a short phase of exponential inflation at early times, after which the dark matter halos started collapsing under their own gravity and grew in a hierarchical manner via merging. This landscape of dark matter potential wells then acted as 'hosts' for the baryons, which condensed into galaxies and started forming the stars, from which we gain the vast majority of our knowledge about the Universe.

Building a Galaxy

There are two main scenarios through which a galaxy is believed to be able to form from dark matter halos (potential wells) and baryons: through hierarchical merging of halos and the associated baryons, and via a monolithic collapse of the baryons in the potential wells.

The hierarchical merging is a direct consequence of the structure formation picture outlined above, where the merging of dark matter structures drags along the baryons and enable these to merger with them. Already in Toomre & Toomre (1972) is was made clear, that some of the observed peculiar galaxies were well described by a merger scenario. Generally, when galaxies merge the end result is a structure with a broad distribution of internal velocities, such that most orbits around the systems center of gravity are occupied.

The monolithic collapse of the baryonic gas in (isolated) galaxies, on the other hand, often results in a preferred rotation of the system. Since baryonic matter can loose its energy by radiating in ways dark matter cannot , the gas residing in the dark matter potential wells will over time loose its energy and slowly sink or condense into the bottom of the potential well. Since angular momentum needs to be conserved, this results in a rotating system where the gas often flattens to a disk-like structure with a preferred direction of rotation. Such a fairly equilibrated system can of course be destroyed or stirred up if it encounters the gravitational effects of another galaxy, or in the most extreme case becomes part of a galaxy merger.

Hence, the merging of dark matter halos and their galaxies combined with the condensation of gas in (isolated) dark matter potential wells are the main drivers of building galaxies, and are able to reproduce the observed population of galaxies. Three classes of galaxies are know: the ellipticals, the spirals and the irregulars. These are often divided into subclasses, or Hubble classes, These classes address the appearance of the galaxies, like eccentricity of the ellipticals, whether a bar is present or not in the spirals, and how tightly wound the spiral's arms are. The formation of galaxies via hierarchical merging preferentially produces ellipticals, whereas the main end-product of a monolithic collapse is a nicely rotating spiral galaxy. The irregular galaxies consist of everything belonging to neither the elliptical nor the spiral Hubble classes, e.g., merger remnants not yet equilibrated or odd-looking truly irregular galaxies.

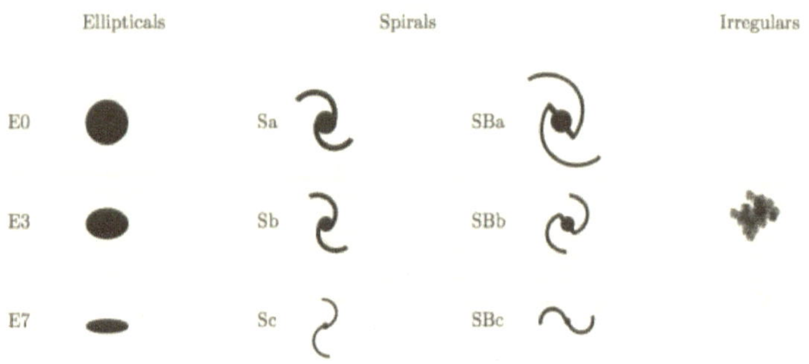

A schematic overview of the Hubble galaxy classes. The left panel shows the elliptical classes of galaxies. They are designated by Ex, with x giving the (observed) eccentricity. The two center panels show the sub-division of spiral galaxies. Spirals are designated with Sα where α refers to how tightly wound the spiral arms are, with 'a' referring to the most tightly wound arms. In the case of prominent bars a B is added. The right hand panel represents irregular galaxies, which consist of everything (including recent merger events) that cannot be categorized as either elliptical (Ex), spiral (Sα), or barred spiral (SBα). Ellipticals are the end product of galaxies formed in recent merger events, whereas spirals need an extended epoch of monolithic collapse of gas to conserve the preferred direction of rotation and the spiral pattern.

It is not only the appearance and the internal velocities of these different galaxies that are significantly different. Also the stellar populations of ellipticals, spirals and irregulars are distinctly different. Since most ellipticals are believed to be the equilibrated end-product of a merging event, most of the stars in the final elliptical were already present prior to the merger, i.e., they are relatively old. On the other hand the condensation of gas in spirals induces new star formation, and hence the age spread of stars in spirals is much broader than in ellipticals. If irregular galaxies are recent mergers that have not yet equilibrated into ellipticals, they might have experienced a recent burst of star formation induced by the collision of gas during merging. Irregulars therefore have a fairly young population of stars. Thus, the population of stars, i.e., the star formation and the merging activity in galaxies is closely linked to each other and are important factors when dealing with galaxy formation and evolution. The epoch where the global star formation rate in the Universe peaked has been estimated to be at $1 < z < 3$. This agrees well with the peak of galaxy merging, and therefore supports this picture. It is not only bursts of star formation the merging of galaxies seems to trigger. Galaxy mergers are also thought to be able to trigger the most violent phase of a galaxies life, the active (quasar) phase, by enabling large amounts of gas to accrete onto a galaxies central black hole.

Galaxies' Active (Quasar) Phase

So far most of the galaxies described have been relaxed equilibrated systems quietly residing in the bottom of cold dark matter potential wells, slowly forming stars from their gas reservoirs. However, this state of peace and quit does not last forever. It is believed that most, if not all, galaxies in their lifetime of several billion years experience one or more short active phases lasting for only ~ 107 years. Galaxies in this phase of their evolution are referred to as active galaxies or 'AGN'. Strictly speaking AGN refers to the cause of the active phase, namely the Active Galactic Nucleus and not the actual galaxy itself. However, it has become standard to refer to active galaxies by this acronym, which we will therefore also do here.

AGN are among the most luminous and powerful objects in the sky. The majority of AGN are known to vary by a few percent over weeks, months and years to the more extreme cases of several percent within a few nights. That some AGN vary on these short time-scales indicate that the variability originates from very small regions of sizes from light-months down to a few light-days(!) across. This early led to the conclusion, that something extremely small and massive must reside at the center of active galaxies. It is generally accepted that a supermassive black hole (SMBH) lives at the center of most, if not all, galaxies.

Several classes of AGN exist. Among these are Seyfert 1 and 2 galaxies named after their discoverer (Seyfert 1943), broad and narrow line radio galaxies (BLRG and NLRG respectively), optically violently variable (OVV) galaxies, BL Lac galaxies, Blazars, lowionization nuclear emission line regions (LINERs), quasi stellar objects (QSOs), and quasars. Some of these names are descriptive for the object class, whereas others are named for historical reasons. Furthermore, the classes are far from clearly distinct. For instance LINERs are thought to be a low-luminosity extension of the Seyfert galaxies, quasar and QSO nowadays refer to the same class, even though they were originally distinct classes, and Blazars are supposed to be the combination of OVVs and BL Lac galaxies. This makes the 'zoology' of AGN a rather complicated matter.

Nevertheless, we attempt to summarized the key features of the different kinds of AGN. This table is by no means exhaustive but gives a good flavor for what characterizes and distinguishes different AGN types.

	Seyfert†		Quasar		Radio Galaxy		Blazar	
	1	2	RL	RQ	BLRG	NLRG	OVV	BL Lac
Broad Lines ($\sigma_v > 1000$ km/s)	+	–*	+	+	+	–	+	–
Narrow Lines ($\sigma_v \sim 100$ km/s)	+	+	+	+	+	+	+	–
Number Density [Mpc^{-3}]	10^{-4}		10^{-7}		10^{-6}			
M_B (classic definition)	$< -21.5 + 5 \log h$		$> -21.5 + 5 \log h$		–		–	
Strongly Polarized > 5% of light							+	+
Significant Radio Emission			+		+	+	+	+
Variable > 1%-level	+	+	+	+	+	+	+	+

The Main AGN Types and Their Characteristics† LINERS are believed to be a low-luminosity extension of the Seyferts.* NGC1068 is an example of a classic Seyfert 2 galaxy, where polarized broad lines are actually observed. This might indicate the presence of an obscured/hidden BLR supporting the unified model of AGN

The sometimes opaque or muddied classification scheme of AGN has given rise to the idea, that the different classes of AGN are in principle the same object perceived differently by the observer due to viewing angle. This unified model for AGN is still a matter of debate, but has to some extent made the AGN classification more digestible.

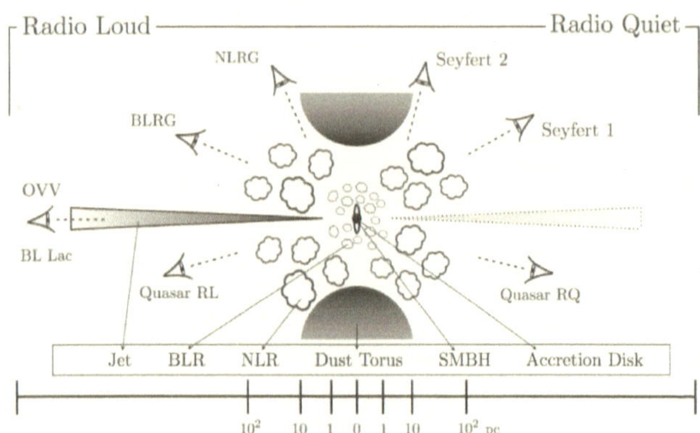

: Illustration of the inner region of an active galaxy. The classes of active galaxies from before diagram are indicated by the viewing angles the unified AGN model predicts them to be observed from. The approximate length-scales are indicated at the bottom. The left hand side contain galaxies with pronounced radio emission, whereas the right hand side galaxies have more modest radio luminosities. Note that the validity of the unified AGN model is still being debated.

AGN are believed to get their power from the SMBH residing in the center of the galaxy. It is believed that the SMBH is swallowing material which radiates strongly, as it falls into the deep potential well of the SMBH from a surrounding accretion disk. This central engine is part of the 6 main components of the unified AGN model.

• Central supermassive black hole (SMBH): The SMBH is assumed to inhabit the bottom of the galaxy's dark matter potential well and be the key part of the central AGN. The SMBH in the (non-AGN) Milky Way has been monitored extensively and has an estimated mass of ~ 10‘6M. This is two orders of magnitude smaller than the average size of AGN SMBHs of ~ 10’8M.

• Accretion disk: A flattened disk of gas and stars rotating around the SMBH. Matter being accreted onto the SMBH from this disk is thought to be the main source of radiation for the extreme AGN luminosities. The accretion disk and the SMBH make up the central AGN engine.

• Broad line region (BLR): A small inner region believed to be less than a few light-years across, composed of individual high density clouds (ρ ~ 10'10cm−3) giving rise to the broad emission line features observed in most AGN spectra. The temperature of the BLR is expected to be TBLR ~ 10'4K.

• Narrow line region (NLR): A wider (~ 50 - 100pc) region giving rise to the narrow lines in the quasar spectra, such as [Oiii]. The density of the NLR is expected to be (ρ ~ 10'6 cm−3). The temperature in the NLR is the same as in the BLR, i.e., TNLR ~ 10'4K.

• Dust Torus: An obscuring dusty torus believed to block the light from the BLR and NLR for near-edge-on galaxy views.

• Jet: Along the rotational axis of the central engine, powerful radio jets (most prominent in the radio loud AGN) form from the synchrotron radiation of the material being accreted onto the SMBH. The most powerful and most variable AGN are seen 'down the barrel' of these jets.

These individual components of the AGN model give rise to some of the characteristic features in AGN spectra (a standard composite AGN (quasar) spectrum). We will described the specific features of the quasar spectrum and how they can be used to probe the physics governing AGN.

Despite the extreme differences in length scales of the different components of the AGN (and galaxies in general), from sub-parsec scales of the central SMBH and accretion disk to the several kpc of the bulge and outer regions of the galaxy itself, there seems to be a remarkable tight correlation between the size of the central black hole and the galaxy observables like for example luminosity, the velocity dispersion and the (bulge) mass of the stars, and light concentration. For example several of these studies find that the black hole mass is tightly correlated with the bulge mass such that MSMBH ~ 0.003 × Mbulge. In the argue that log(M'SMBH/M) ~ 8.18 + 1.55 × (log(M'tot/M) − 13.0) with Mtot being the total galaxy (halo) mass, i.e., they argue that a standard AGN SMBH of 108M approximately corresponds to 10−5Mtot. Whether these scaling relations are due to a causal co-evolution of the galaxy and its SMBH across the vastly different length scales or a simple consequence of ΛCDM hierarchical merging is debated.

Quasars – AGN at Its Best

One of the most powerful and brightest kind of AGN is the quasar. Quasars5 have extreme luminosities corresponding to absolute magnitudes of Mr ~ −24 making quasars the second brightest objects in the sky only outshone by a few gamma ray bursts as illustrated in Figure. Quasars are observed out to redshifts of 6 , and even at redshift 7 they have been found, showing that they had already formed and started shining less than a 1 Gyr year after the Big Bang. This puts strong constraints on theories trying to describe the physics of quasars and AGN

Even though quasars have been observed at z ~ 7 the distribution of quasars peaks at redshifts 2–3. Also the co-moving density of quasars peaks a these redshifts. The fact that quasars were more common at earlier epochs speaks in favor of the scenario, where many AGN and quasars are triggered by gravitational interaction and merging of galaxies mentioned. Since the merger rate between galaxies was higher, than it is today, at these redshifts, naturally more quasars would be observed per co-moving volume if they are a consequence of interactions. That the average quasar density drops at higher redshift is explained by the fact that in a ΛCDM Universe there were very few galaxies with masses high enough to host the SMBHs of quasars at z > 3 − 4.

CHAPTER TWO

Selecting Quasars via Variability

The name "quasars" started out as short for "quasi-stellar radio sources" (here "quasi-stellar" means "sort of like stars"). The discovery of radio sources that appeared point-like, just like stars, came with the use of surplus World War II radar equipment in the 1950s. Although few astronomers would have predicted it, the sky turned out to be full of strong sources of radio waves. As they improved the images that their new radio telescopes could make, scientists discovered that some radio sources were in the same location as faint blue "stars." No known type of star in our Galaxy emits such powerful radio radiation. What then were these "quasi-stellar radio sources"?

In 1963 at Caltech's Palomar Observatory, Maarten Schmidt was puzzling over the spectrum of one of the radio stars, which was named 3C 273 because it was the 273rd entry in the third Cambridge catalog of radio sources. There were strong emission lines in the spectrum, and Schmidt recognized that they had the same spacing between them as the Balmer lines of hydrogen (see Radiation and Spectra). But the lines in 3C 273 were shifted far to the red of the wavelengths at which the Balmer lines are normally located. Indeed, these lines were at such long wavelengths that if the redshifts were attributed to the Doppler effect, 3C 273 was receding from us at a speed of 45,000 kilometers per second, or about 15% the speed of light! Since stars don't show Doppler shifts this large, no one had thought of considering high redshifts to be the cause of the strange spectra.

Quasar Pioneers and Quasar 3C 273. (a) Maarten Schmidt (left), who solved the puzzle of the quasar spectra in 1963, shares a joke in this 1987 photo with Allan Sandage, who took the first spectrum of a quasar. Sandage was also instrumental in measuring the value of Hubble's constant. (b) This is the first quasar for which a redshift was measured. The redshift showed that the light from it took about 2.5 billion years to reach us. Despite this great distance, it is still one of the quasars closest to the Milky Way Galaxy. Note also the faint streak going toward the upper left from the quasar. Some quasars, like 3C 273, eject super-fast jets of material. The jet from 3C 273 is about 200,000 light-years long.

The puzzling emission lines in other star-like radio sources were then reexamined to see if they, too, might be well-known lines with large redshifts. This proved to be the case, but the other objects were found to be receding from us at even greater speeds. Their astounding speeds showed that the radio "stars" could not possibly be stars in our own Galaxy. Any true star moving at more than a few hundred kilometers per second would be able to overcome the gravitational pull of the Galaxy and completely escape from it. (As we shall see later in this chapter, astronomers eventually discovered that there was also more to these "stars" than just a point of light.)

It turns out that these high-velocity objects only look like stars because they are compact and very far away. Later, astronomers discovered objects with large redshifts that appear star-like but have no radio emission. Observations also showed that quasars were bright in the infrared and X-ray bands too, and not all these X-ray or infrared-bright quasars could be seen in either the radio or the visible-light bands of the spectrum. Today, all these objects are referred to as quasi-stellar objects (QSOs), or, as they are more popularly known, quasars. (The name was also soon appropriated by a manufacturer of home electronics.)

Typical Quasar Imaged by the Hubble Space Telescope. One of these two bright "stars" in the middle is in our Galaxy, while the other is a quasar 9 billion light-years away. From this picture alone, there's no way to say which is which. (The quasar is the one in the center of the picture.) (credit: Charles Steidel (CIT)/NASA/ESA)

In the record-holding quasars, the first Lyman series line of hydrogen, with a laboratory wavelength of 121.5 nanometers in the ultraviolet portion of the spectrum, is shifted all the way through the visible region to the infrared. At such high redshifts, the simple formula for converting a Doppler shift to speed (Radiation and Spectra) must be modified to take into account the effects of the theory of relativity. If we apply the relativistic form of the Doppler shift formula, we find that these redshifts correspond to velocities of about 96% of the speed of light.

In this we present a new and simple technique for selecting extensive, complete and pure quasar samples, based on their intrinsic variability. We parametrize the single-band variability by a power-law model for the light-curve structure function, with amplitude A and power-law index γ. We show that quasars can be efficiently separated from other non-variable and variable sources by the location of the individual sources in the A–γ plane. We use ~60 epochs of imaging data, taken over ~8 years, from SDSS Stripe 82, to demonstrate the power of variability as a quasar classifier in multi-epoch surveys. For UV excess selected objects, variability performs just as well as the standard SDSS color selection, identifying quasars with a completeness of 90% and a purity of 95%. In the redshift range $2.5 < z < 3$, where color selection is known to be problematic, variability can select quasars with a completeness of 90% and a purity of 96%. This is a factor of 5-10 times more pure than existing color-selection of quasars in this redshift range. Selecting objects from a broad griz color box without UV excess information, variability selection in Stripe 82 can afford completeness and purity of 92%, despite a factor of 30 more contaminants than quasars in the color-selected feeder sample. We also show that even with much sparser time sampling, e.g., with just 6 epochs over 3 years as is the case for Pan-STARRS 1, variability is still an encouragingly efficient quasar classifier. Finally, we show that the presented A–γ technique, besides selecting quasars is also efficient at selecting (periodic) variable objects such as RR Lyrae.

– *Prologue* –

Quasars are some of the most versatile astronomical objects known. First and foremost, they are interesting themselves. For example, samples of quasars provide precise measurements of the evolution and spectral properties of AGN in general and quasars in particular. As described before about AGN and quasars probe galaxy evolution in general and especially at the epoch where the galaxy merger rate peaked and most stars formed. But not only do quasar samples provide us with insight into the nature (and nurture) of galaxy evolution and map the black hole growth in the centers of galaxies, they are also the key to various other areas of astrophysics. In particular the clustering of quasars is a tracer of mass clustering on both large and small scales and hence carries information about intergalactic structure formation. Quasar sight lines probe the content of the intergalactic medium as well as individual structures in absorption. Hence, they provide information on quasar environments and the quasar emission geometry, and shed light on the physical nature of Lyman limit systems and damped Lyα systems . If quasars are also gravitationally magnified by a lens, exploration of the dark matter (halo) content of galaxies, gaining knowledge about the molecular gas content in distant galaxies and using the integrated Sachs-Wolfe effect by cross correlating quasars with the CMB to obtain estimates of cosmological parameters and the dark energy equation of state becomes possible. In summary: large well-defined quasar samples are a cornerstone of observational cosmology.

Many applications rely on large statistical samples of quasars. Photometric quasar samples have recently grown to nearly a million objects (850,000 actual quasars). Despite these impressive catalog sizes, which at first glance might seem overwhelming, the number statistics still limits the achievable science in several of the science cases mentioned above; especially those where particular, and hence rare, geometric constellations of quasars are needed. For instance a 3σ detection of a luminositydependent quasar bias above z & 1.9 when analyzing the angular clustering of quasars, needs an estimated sample size of at least 1,200,000 actual quasars. Searches for binary quasars, which provide interesting knowledge about small scale clustering and hence shed light on quasar triggering mechanisms and the nature of quasar progenitors, also needs to be based on samples with > 106 actual quasars in order to obtain reasonably sized statistical samples of possible quasar pairs. Also quasar-galaxy clustering exploring the statistics of quasars behind the foreground galaxies, calls for larger (relatively low-z) quasar samples than exist today.

Furthermore, exploring the 'transverse proximity effect' in the Lyα forest of quasars, with foreground quasars near the sight line of background quasars is presently limited by quasar sample sizes. Obtaining larger photometric quasar catalogs to boost possible candidates for spectroscopic follow-up is needed. The size estimates of the cosmological parameters and the dark energy equation of state will also be improved by larger photometric samples of $1<z<5$ quasars. Last but not least, larger photometric quasar catalogs will enhance the number of known gravitationally lensed quasars. At present only ~100 quasar lenses are known. A larger sample of the rare gravitationally lensed quasar systems will, among other things, improve our knowledge about cosmology, galaxy mass distributions, quasar hosts and the growth of the host's central black holes.

Hence, pursuing large well-defined quasar samples is not only crucial for investigating the quasars themselves, but provides the data for a large palette of interesting astrophysical applications. The main purpose of this chapter is to investigate a new approach for obtaining such quasar samples in the future. Previous efforts have focused mainly on purely photometric selection of quasars as we will describe below. We will present an alternate approach to selecting quasars, based on their intrinsic variability. This is an important step towards understanding how quasars are selected in the most efficient and powerful way in future time-domain surveys, where color-selection may not be the preferred selection method. We will illustrate that it is actually feasible to take advantage of the intrinsic variability of quasars to select them, and show how this in practice can be applied to future time-domain surveys focusing mainly on the Pan-STARRS 1 survey which is already well underway. To sum up:

Huge well-defined quasar samples serve as a versatile cornerstone of observational cosmology; current samples are still not large enough for many applications.

Igniting Galaxies – The Quasar (AGN) Engine

The central engine of AGN is generally believed to be an accretion disk dumping material onto a super-massive black hole (SMBH). In this section we will describe this picture in a bit more detail, before we take advantage of one of its main characteristics, variability in the produced radiation, to select quasars from time-domain data. The fueling of the central engine is a complicated process, which is probably best illustrated by the schematic overview of the fueling of central black holes and the possible formation of SMBHs from Shlosman et al. (1990). We will not attempt to describe every step in the fueling process, but only outline the crucial physical consideration one needs to take into account, and refer to Shlosman and their references for a more in-depth description of AGN fueling mechanisms.

Igniting a galaxy, i.e., enabling gas to accrete onto the sub-parsec sized SMBH (region) so it starts radiating, faces some theoretical challenges. First of all the SMBH needs to form and exist in the center of the galaxy before it can start radiating. In the lowredshift Universe there have been plenty of time to merge galaxies and black holes to form SMBHs in the centers of gaseous galaxies, however, as AGN are found out to redshift 7. This implies that whatever process forms black holes in the very early Universe, either via the collapse of super-massive isolated stars or by merging and accretion onto neutron stars, needs to be able to produce black hole 'seeds' that can grow to masses of 10‘8M via accretion in gaseous galaxies in less than ~ 5×10’8 years, if SMBH are indeed residing at the centers of AGN. It has been argued that it is possible to form black hole seeds of masses 100 – 200M at very high redshifts, possibly leaving just enough time for them to grow into SMBH before $z = 7$. This is under the assumption that both a large enough dark matter halo to host the black hole seed and the gas needed for it to grow, is available. Since the SMBHs usually only correspond to ~10−5 of the total halo mass, a dark matter halo of the order 10‘8M/10−5 = 10’13M needs to be available at $z > 7$ to ignite AGN, putting further constraints on the AGN models as well as ΛCDM.

Another challenge in establishing an AGN is, that when the SMBH is formed in the center of the galaxy an accretion flow onto it needs to be established. One difficulty with this is, for example, that a given black hole mass has a maximum luminosity it can radiate with under the assumption of a spherically symmetric system. This limiting luminosity, known as the Eddington luminosity, LEdd, is a balance between the gravitational force the SMBH acts with on the in-falling gas, and the radiation pressure the gas produces as

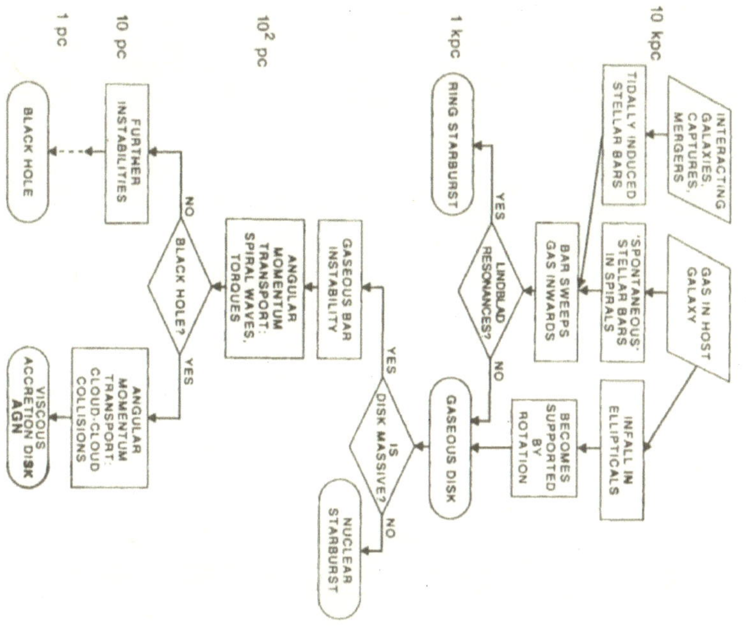

Schematic overview of the possibly ways of fueling the central black hole of an AGN or quasar illustrating its complicated nature.

it accretes onto the SMBH. If the radiation pressure is given by

$$P_{\rm rad}(r) = \frac{L}{4\pi r^2 c}\,, \tag{2.1}$$

assuming that the gas is ionized and the scattering of photons on the electrons has the Thomson cross section, $\sigma_{\rm T}$, the force the radiation acts with is described by

$$F_{\rm rad} = \sigma_{\rm T} P_{\rm rad}(r) n_e(r)\,, \tag{2.2}$$

with ne being the electron density. If this force is smaller than the gravitational force on the gas, the infall will be successful. On the other hand if

$$F_{\text{rad}} \geq F_{\text{grav}} = \frac{GM_{\text{SMBH}}\,\rho(r)}{r^2},$$

Equation (2.3)

where ρ(r) is the density of the gas cloud surrounding the SMBH, the radiation will prevent more matter from being accreted. This mechanism is 'self-regulating': The amount of radiation will decrease until the gravity is strong enough to accrete matter again, then the radiation pressure will increase until it turns off accretion and radiation then decreases again, and so on. This balance defines the Eddington luminosity and combining Equations (2.1)–(2.3) give that

$$L_{\text{Edd}} \equiv \frac{4\pi cG\rho(r)}{\sigma_{\text{T}} n_e} M_{\text{SMBH}} \approx 1.26 \times 10^{46} \left(\frac{M_{\text{SMBH}}}{10^8 M_\odot}\right) \frac{\text{erg}}{\text{s}},$$

where ρ(r)/ne corresponds to the proton mass, mp, assuming that the gas consist mostly of ionized hydrogen. This shows that in the case of spherical accretion a bright quasar with a luminosity of ~ 1046 erg s could be powered by a SMBH of 108M. The Eddington luminosity hence gives the maximum luminosity an object can obtain via spherical accretion. Super-Eddington luminosities have been observed in several quasars This is possible because the central accretion in AGN is (obviously) not spherical.

The Eddington luminosity also puts a constraint on the accretion rate needed. Formally luminosity is accretion rate in units of c 2 , i.e., E/t = mc2 /t. Assuming that the fixed efficiency of converting the mass accreted onto the SMBH into radiation, η, is of the order 0.1, the highest possible accretion rate in the spherically symmetric model, know as the Eddington accretion rate, becomes:

$$\dot{M}_{\rm Edd} = \frac{L_{\rm Edd}}{c^2\eta} \approx 2.2\left(\frac{M_{\rm SMBH}}{10^8 M_\odot}\right)\left(\frac{\eta}{0.1}\right)^{-1} \frac{M_\odot}{\rm yr} .$$

Thus the size of the SMBH regulates the maximum allowed accretion. According to this, an accretion rate of ~ 2M/yr is needed to power a quasar with L ~ 1046erg/s. Even though the spherical Eddington accretion picture gives a simple theoretical framework for the central engine, it is by no means a sufficient description. It is a big challenge to theoretically obtain continuous (semi)stable accretion rates of this order to power the AGN, and hence, an important step of any AGN model is to collect enough gas to sustain the accretion for the expected lifetime of the AGN. Finding the gas is usually not a big problem, as most galaxies contain several factors more gas in the interstellar medium than needed for the accretion. The real challenge is to transport the gas from the interstellar medium of the galaxy all the way into the SMBH sub-parsec scales. This gas-funneling needs to transport a significant amount of the gas' angular momentum elsewhere, for it to reach these extremely small scales, and to make sure the gas has the right temperature to prevent kinetic gas-pressure from limiting the gas-flow and lowering the accretion rate.

One way of lowering the angular momentum of the gas, sometimes by as much as a factor of 104, is by interacting gravitationally with other galaxies. As mentioned briefly in merging of galaxies (both minor and major) are believed to be able to enhance the fueling of AGN, or even trigger AGN. In simulations it has been investigated whether gravitational interaction of galaxies is capable of bringing the acquired amount of gas into the SMBH region and ignite quasars. Most studies indicate that this is indeed the case, but due to the extreme difference in length scale (from kpc to sub-parsec) it is still debatable whether merging can bring the gas so close to the SMBH that the actual accretion happens. Also observational evidence for merger activity in AGN has been established. Whether it is a necessity for AGN to have been gravitationally interacting to ignite has been a matter of great debate. However, in the most recent studies strong arguments are presented, that mergers are no necessity for galaxies to ignite, even though mergers do seem to be able to trigger AGN in some cases. A second possibility for gas to loose its angular momentum is by spontaneous instability caused by interaction of the accretion disk with other parts of the galaxy, minor interactions or super nova explosions. Hence, it seems to be possible for galaxies to ignite and enter their quasar (AGN) phase both with and without external gravitational interaction, as also shown in the top part of Shlosman's flow-chart

A natural consequence of the simple model for the central engine described here, is that the accretion rate is not necessarily constant or stable. The temperature of the in-falling gas might change, resulting in an altered spectral shape of the radiation, the Eddington limit might be reached, the amount of gas funneled onto the SMBH by a recent merger might run out, or blobs in the accretion flow could be swallowed irregularly by the SMBH, etc. Hence, it must be expected that the luminosity of AGN varies. As noted in Table basically all AGN have indeed been observed to vary. In particular the variability of quasars has been studied in great detail. Quasars are observed to exhibit brightness variations, of typically & 10% over several years. Even though accretion disk instabilities has so far been the most prevailing model for the quasar (AGN) variability, several other physical processes are and have been discussed as other important causes of the observed variability. For instance, it has been suggested that large-scale changes in the amount of in-falling material may be important, as well as starbursts in the host galaxy, micro lensing by the host galaxy and compact dark matter object and stochasticity of multiple supernovae.

Irrespective of the physics behind the variability, it is an observational fact that quasars vary significantly over periods of years. This variability has been exploited for several purposes, e.g., to estimate Eddington ratios and black hole masses.

Apart from determining Eddington ratios and black hole masses and constraining the physics of AGN, another potentially very powerful application of the observed quasar variability is to identify quasars. With for example the Sloan digital sky survey, the quasar equatorial survey team and the optical gravitational lensing experiment, large-scale, multiepoch and multi-band surveys have emerged, and have been used to search for quasars. The Panoramic Survey Telescope & Rapid Response System 1 and 4, and the Large Synoptic Survey Telescope will take such surveys to the next level. Even though all these surveys have multi-epoch data, the largest quasar samples stem from color and not variability selection. The characteristic so-called 'UV excess' of quasars, their bright blue SDSS u–g color for instance, is capable of separating the quasars from their stellar contaminants in color-color space, allowing for efficient selection of targets for spectroscopic follow-up. Such UV excess color selection is, however, only efficient for low (z . 2.5) and high (z & 3) redshift quasars, since the quasar and stellar loci overlap in the $u - g$ color for $2.5 < z < 3.0$ objects, causing the selection efficiency (or purity) in that region to drop below 50%. For quasars with $2.6 < z < 2.8$ the UV excess color selection efficiency is close to 10%. This confusion reigns until the Ly-break of high-z quasars moves into the g-band and again makes for unusual colors.

Moreover, u-band imaging is expensive: the area and depth of an optical imaging survey can be greatly increased by focusing on redder filters, where atmospheric attenuation is lower and detectors more efficient. For example, the Pan-STARRS 1 telescope offers the possibility of creating the largest sample of quasars to date with its multi-epoch 30,000 deg2 (3/4 of the sky) grizY imaging survey named '3π'. For the purpose of identifying quasars in this data set, the question remains, whether we can compensate for the lack of u-band data by exploiting the multi-epoch nature of the imaging instead. With one eye on the potential of Pan-STARRS 1, we therefore explore the possibilities of creating large, complete and pure samples of quasars based on limited color information, but with light curves spanning several years. We use Stripe 82 of SDSS as a testbed, both for the method in general and for making mock Pan-STARRS 1 data sets.

Variability Characterization of Sources and the Structure Function

Color Selection

The most common way to generate large samples of optical quasar candidates for followup is by specifying a particular region of interest in color space, as it was done in for example SDSS. For quasars at $z < 3$ the $u - g$ color is crucial in this approach since it enables a photometric separation of the quasar candidates from the stellar locus, reducing the number of contaminating objects to a point where spectroscopic follow-up is feasible. This is illustrated in Figure, where we have plotted the median color of ~9000 spectroscopically confirmed quasars, as well as an illustrative comparison sample of 5000 F/G and 483 RR Lyrae stars, all drawn from the SDSS Stripe 82 photometric catalog DR7. The top panels and the bottom left panel of Figure shows the distribution of the samples in the color-color planes of the SDSS ugriz color cube. This clearly shows the power of the $u - g$ color (upper left panel) compared to the $g - r$, $r - i$ and $i - z$ colors in separating the quasars from their contaminants, especially for low-redshift quasars.

The color magnitude diagram in the lower right panel illustrates that a cut in magnitude will also eliminate contaminants. The contours indicate the stellar locus of Stripe 82 point sources with $15 < r < 18$. For higher redshift objects (z & 2.5, shown as magenta points in Figure) the quasars intersect the stellar locus (top left panel). The purity for $2.5 < z < 3.0$ quasar candidate samples is around 10-50% in the color-selected SDSS quasar target sample. In general the color selection method is efficient for low and high redshift quasars, but for the intermediate redshift objects contamination becomes a severe problem.

With Pan-STARRS 1 the contamination problem is even more pronounced when using the color selection method only. Pan-STARRS 1 has a 5-filter system consisting of SDSS-like g, r, i, z bands (albeit with significantly higher red sensitivity) and a Y filter. The crucial $u - g$ color used in the SDSS color selection method is not available: the contamination of a color-selected Pan-STARRS 1 quasar sample will be a problem for $z > 2.5$ as well as for $z < 2.5$. It is therefore necessary to find a way of separating the majority of quasars from the contaminating stellar locus in order to obtain a pure Pan-STARRS 1 quasar sample. The intrinsic variability of the quasars described (and their contaminants) is a very promising tool for doing this.

Source variability: power-law structure functions

The structure function characterizes the variability of quasars (and the other sources) by quantifying the variability amplitude as a function of the time lag between compared observations. For any object the observables for estimating the structure function are the N(N−1) 2 data pairs, assuming N light curve data points, describing the variability as the magnitude difference between two epochs i and j, corrected for measurement errors, i.e.,

$$V_{i,j}(\Delta t_{i,j}) = \Delta m_{i,j} - \sqrt{\sigma_i^2 + \sigma_j^2}\,.$$

Here Δmi, j is the measured magnitude difference between observation i and j. The σi and σj are the photometric errors on the measurements and Δti, j is the time difference between the two observations. The quantity V is defined like this so that its average, over a large number of data pairs, is an estimator for the intrinsic standard deviation of the source magnitude.

At this point we note that Δti, j usually refers to the time lag in the quasar rest frame. However, computing this requires a priori knowledge of the quasar redshift, and when

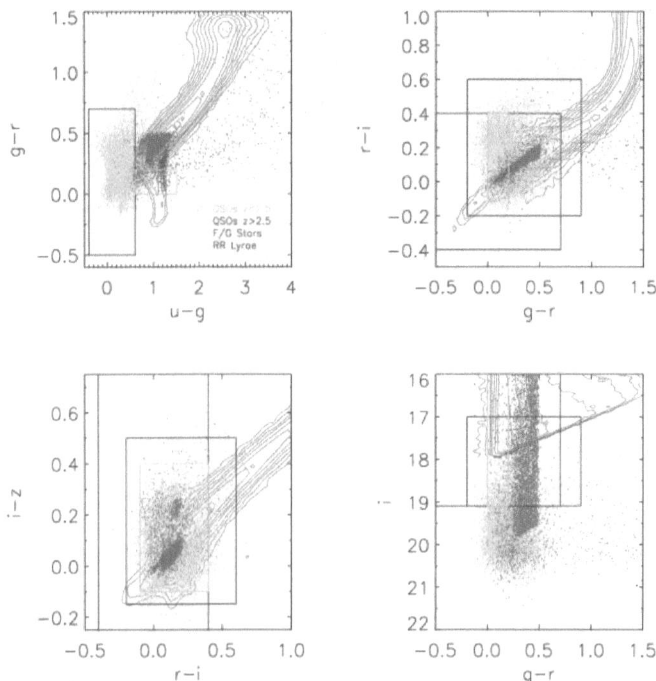

Projections of point-source colors from the SDSS Stripe 82 data described to the ugriz color space. The light blue (magenta) points show z < 2.5 (z > 2.5) spectroscopically confirmed quasars. Illustrative contaminant point sources are shown as grey (F/G stars) and red (RR Lyrae) points. These panels demonstrate the importance of the u-band data in color selection of quasars, with the u – g color allowing the clearest discrimination. This clearly shows the necessity for an alternative way to lower the amount of contamination when the filters are too red. The lower right color magnitude diagram illustrates that a cut in magnitude will also eliminate some contaminants, and is included for comparison purposes The narrow appearance of the contaminant sample in the upper right panel is due to our contaminants being mostly reference stars with small photometric errors. The stellar locus spanned by all point sources in Stripe 82 with 15 < r < 18 is shown as the black contours.

selecting objects in imaging-only surveys, we do not know the object redshift. Therefore, we work with time lags in the observed frame. This necessary convention differs from most of the quasar variability literature; we will make some comparisons.

In previous analyses, the average V has been calculated in n time lag bins using data pairs from many quasars, thus 'stacking' the variability signal to allow the properties of the quasar population to be probed. Then

$$V(\Delta t) = \left\langle \sqrt{\frac{\pi}{2}}|\Delta m_{i,j}| - \sqrt{\sigma_i^2 + \sigma_j^2} \right\rangle_{\Delta t},$$

where the average, h i∆t , is taken over all epoch pairs i, j, whose lag falls in the bin ∆t. The same approach can be taken in estimating the structure function of classes of objects if, say, only two epochs are available per object, but large samples exist in that case the Equation becomes an ensemble average. Others find that the ensemble average quasar structure function appears to follow an increasing power law with time lag.

On the other hand, for the case where the light curve sampling of each object is high, we can compute the average V(∆t) for an individual object. Binning the N(N−1) 2 data pairs from an object's N-point light curve gives an estimate of V(∆t) defined at each bin center. This approach is computationally efficient, and provides a free-form view of the object's structure function. However, in the case of relatively sparse sampled data (6 epochs over 3 years in the Pan-STARRS 1 3π survey), binning the data pairs to obtain the structure function from Equation to estimate the variability may not be the optimal approach.

In Equation, both the noise and the intrinsic photometric variability are assumed (implicitly) to have a Gaussian distribution. We can then extend this simple model of quasar variability to include a power law increase in variability with time lag.

$$V_{\mathrm{mod}}(\Delta t_{i,j}|A,\gamma) = A\left(\frac{\Delta t_{i,j}}{1\mathrm{yr}}\right)^{\gamma} .$$

We can then fit this model to a given set of data, (Δmi, j , Δti, j), as follows. We write the likelihood for the power law parameters A and γ as

$$\mathcal{L}(A,\gamma) = \prod_{i,j} L_{i,j} ,$$

assuming a set of independent magnitude differences as our data. Here Li, j is the likelihood of observing one particular magnitude difference Δmi, j between two light curve points separated by Δti, j . Following the ensemble analyses referred to above, we assume an underlying Gaussian distribution of Δm values and Gaussian photometric errors:

$$L_{ij} = \frac{1}{\sqrt{2\pi \mathrm{V}^2_{\mathrm{eff},ij}}} \exp\left(-\frac{\Delta m^2_{ij}}{2\mathrm{V}^2_{\mathrm{eff},ij}}\right) .$$

Here, the effective (observed) variability Veff is

$$V^2_{\mathrm{eff},ij} = V_{\mathrm{mod}}(\Delta t_{ij}|A,\gamma)^2 + \left(\sigma_i^2 + \sigma_j^2\right),$$

we propagate the photometric errors σi and σj by adding them in quadrature to the variability 'error' Vmod(Δti j|A, γ).

This approach can yield posterior probability distributions on the two model parameters, A and γ. The amplitude A quantifies the root-mean-square magnitude difference on a 1 year timescale, while γ is the logarithmic gradient of this mean change in magnitude. We assign uninformative priors for the parameters (uniform in the logarithm of A, and uniform in the arctangent of γ – since γ represents the slope of a straight line), and then explore the posterior probability distribution for these two power law parameters via a simple Markov chain Monte Carlo (MCMC) code. All we are doing is replacing n binned structure function parameters (the values of V in each of the n bins) with two parameters that define a power law structure function, and then inferring these parameters instead of constructing estimators for them. We will show that using a power law model for the variability actually provides a good fit.

SDSS Stripe 82: a Testbed for Variability Studies

We note that to detect and quantify intrinsic quasar variability will likely require multi-epoch data spanning several years. Before surveys with facilities such as Pan-STARRS and LSST become fully available, SDSS Stripe 82 forms an excellent training set and methodological test bed. In this section we will describe the various Stripe 82 data sets that we have created in order to test and illustrate the prospects of our algorithm. The SDSS Stripe 82 region covers approximately 300 deg2 , from right ascension around 300◦ to 60◦

in a 2.5 ◦ wide band on the celestial equator. Over 8 observing seasons it has been repeatedly observed in the fall months, resulting in many epochs (typically ~60) in each of the 5 SDSS bands. As the Pan-STARRS 1 3π survey will contain fewer epochs,

we can 'down-sample' the Stripe 82 object light curves to simulate observations taken with Pan-STARRS 1 (albeit ones at lower angular resolution and depth). Relative to Pan-STARRS 1, Stripe 82 does have the advantage of u–g color coverage, and extensive bright object spectroscopy. One can therefore construct quite pure samples of quasars, RR Lyrae and so on, that may serve as ground truth for our variability selection. In the following subsections we describe the various subsamples used in our study in some detail, and provide a brief overview here. We have selected all the spectroscopically confirmed quasars in Stripe 82 together with a representative set of (stellar locus) contaminants, which contains non-varying (type F/G stars) as well as varying (RR Lyrae) point sources to illustrate our method and algorithm prospects. These objects' photometry data are plotted in ugriz color space. To investigate the selection of quasars by their colors, we define three color selection boxes and explore the objects returned by each. One of these mimics the more limited color selection possible with PanSTARRS 1.

We describe two preparatory steps for turning the ~ 60 epoch Stripe 82 data into a testbed for color plus variability based quasar selection in SDSS (Stripe 82) and Pan-STARRS 1: first, we describe the definition of various sub-sets of candidate objects; then we describe some technical steps 'cleaning' the light curves and down-sampling the Stripe 82 data to mimic Pan-STARRS 1 observations.

Spectroscopically confirmed quasars in Stripe 82

A key to designing a quasar variability selection algorithm is an understanding of the variability properties of objects that are spectroscopically confirmed to be quasars. We have selected all of these (both point sources and extended objects) published in the

SDSS DR5 quasar catalog that fall within Stripe 82. There are 9157 spectroscopically confirmed DR5 quasars in Stripe 82, spanning a redshift range from 0.08 to 5.09. These quasars have $15.4 < i < 22.0$ with a mean of 19.5.

To get the multi-epoch photometry (light curves) for the 9157 quasars we performed an SQL neighbor search in the Stripe 82 DR7 database, choosing a search radius of 0.5 00 to minimize the light curve contamination from misidentified (spatial) neighbors. This search on average yielded 60 epochs per object, after selecting only entries with good BRIGHT, EDGE, BLENDED, NODEBLEND, SATUR, PEAKCENTER, NOTCHECKED, INTERP_CENTER and DEBLEND_NOPEAK flags.

From that we created a set of F/G star colored objects, presumably non-varying, by applying a color-magnitude cut on the standard star catalog so that $0.2 < g - r < 0.48$ and $14.0 < g < 20.2$ for all the objects. This is a suitable cut for F/G stars according to the SEGUE team and makes them potential quasar contaminants because of their $g - r$ color (see Figure). We took a randomly selected subsample of 5000 objects from this catalog and did a neighbor search in Stripe 82 to get multi-epoch observations of these contaminants. We again used a search radius of 0.5 00 and again made sure that none of the flags listed were set.

To be able to test whether our algorithm is able to separate quasars from known variable contaminants, we used the largest available sample of securely identified RR Lyrae within Stripe 82, which consists of 483 RR Lyrae.

UV excess (UVX) objects

We would also like to test our ability to detect quasars in the absence of spectroscopic data. To this end, we defined three photometrically-selected samples of Stripe 82 objects, whose variability properties we will explore. The first of these is defined by a three-dimensional ugri color box in which the SDSS quasar sample is complete for extinction-corrected i magnitudes brighter than 19.1. This color box is given , and is shown with black lines. Note that this selection uses the SDSS u-band data. We extracted all point sources within Stripe 82 that obeyed these 'UV excess' (UVX) criteria. This returned a catalog of 2912 UVX point sources.

-0.4 <	$u-g$	< 0.6
-0.5 <	$g-r$	< 0.7
-0.4 <	$r-i$	< 0.4
	i	< 19.1

Non-UV excess (nUVX) objects

As a compliment to the UVX object sample defined above, where the color selection is known to efficiently return quasars at high completeness, a catalog of 'non-UVX' (nUVX) objects was created from a region of ugriz color space where color selection of quasars is known to have problems. In this particular color box, the quasar locus, containing mostly intermediate redshift (2.5 < z < 3) quasars, crosses the stellar locus. The color selection therefore has efficiency as low as 10% in this region of color space. In the nUVX color box we find 3258 objects in Stripe 82.

$0.6 <$	$u-g$	< 1.5
$0.0 <$	$g-r$	< 0.2
$-0.1 <$	$r-i$	< 0.4
$-0.1 <$	$i-z$	< 0.4
	i	< 19.1

Quasar Candidate Color Selection without u-band Data

To simulate approximately the anticipated Pan-STARRS 1 3π survey light curves, we defined a third color box suitable for a first cut of the Pan-STARRS 1 catalog. The main purpose of this selection (where no u-band information is used) is to excise the quasar locus as it threads through the three-dimensional griz color space. However, part of the stellar locus also lies in this box. We restrict ourselves to right ascensions between 0 and 20 degrees (enclosing a sixth of the Stripe 82 area, ~50 deg2) in order to return a manageable catalog of 12,714 objects. The griz box is indicated by the blue solid lines and is defined in Table. The magnitude cut of 19.1 is chosen to allow straightforward comparison with the UVX and nUVX boxes.

$-0.2 <$	$g-r$	< 0.9
$-0.2 <$	$r-i$	< 0.6
$-0.15 <$	$i-z$	< 0.5
$17 <$	i	< 19.1

Eliminating light curve 'outliers' in Stripe 82

Plotting the complete Stripe 82 multi-epoch photometry output for the various objects revealed some outlying points that were several magnitudes fainter than adjacent flux points; only some of these outliers were found to be caused by image defects. However, we assume that such a significant decrease in magnitude in a single observation must be non-physical. We therefore removed the outliers (irrespective of their origin) by running a median filter on the photometric measurements. Measurements with a residual between the medianized light curve and the photometric data larger than 0.25 magnitudes were removed. In Figure we show the g, r and i-band multi-epoch photometric measurements (open symbols indicating the removed measurements) with the corresponding medianized light curves over-plotted for quasar SDSS J203817.37+003029.8. The bottom panel shows the residuals, with the limit of 0.25 magnitudes indicated by the dashed lines. As is the case here, in general, only a small fraction of the epochs is removed.

It is these cleaned multi-epoch measurements, where the outlying observations have been removed, we use in the determination and exploration of the objects' variability.

Down-sampling Stripe 82 light curves to the Pan-STARRS 1 cadence

In order to explore quasar selection in the context of the Pan-STARRS 1 3π survey, we down-sampled the Stripe 82 data to mimic the Pan-STARRS 1 observations. We assumed 3 observing seasons for Pan-STARRS 1, with a duration of 155 days (covering all filters) each. Only Stripe 82 objects with more than 7 epochs in each (SDSS) season were passed to the actual down-sampling routine:

~1% of the quasars, < 0.1% of the F/G stars and ~20% of the RR Lyrae did not satisfy this criteria.

We down-sampled the Stripe 82 light curve data by matching each season of observations

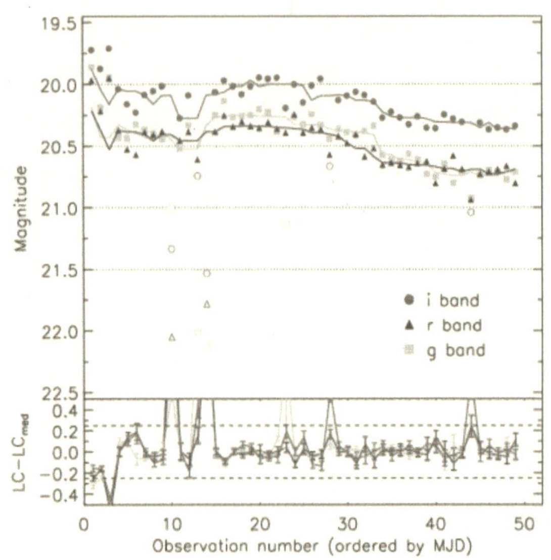

Multi-epoch photometry output from SDSS Stripe 82 for the spectroscopically confirmed quasar SDSS J203817.37+003029.8, shown in the g (green squares), r (blue triangles) and i (red circles) bands. For a handful of epochs, the output magnitudes appear spuriously faint; their inclusion would severely affect the calculation of a variability structure function. Overplotted are the corresponding medianized light curves used to remove the outliers (open symbols) from the raw multi-epoch output. The dotted lines are plotted to guide the eye and are spaced by half a magnitude from 20 to 21.5. In the lower panel the residuals between the medianized light curve and the photometric measurements for the three bands are shown, with the photometric errors over-plotted. The limit used to remove the outliers (|LC − LCmed| > 0.25) is indicated by the horizontal dashed lines.

for the g, r, i and z-band with the (approximately) correct time intervals between consecutive observations in each band. No color information went into the down-sampling. After identifying 6 suitable Stripe 82 epochs in each band we removed all other observations, providing a set of mock Pan-STARRS 1 data.

Date (days)	-60	.	.	.	.	.	-30	.	.	.	.	.	0	5	10	.	.	.	30	35	40	.	.	.	60	.	.	.	.	.	90
Band	*z*	.	.	.	.	.	*Y*	.	.	.	.	.	*i*	*r*	*g*	.	.	.	*i*	*r*	*g*	.	.	.	*Y*	.	.	.	.	.	*z*
Moon	F	.	.	N	.	.	F	.	.	N	.	.	F	.	.	N	.	.	F	.	.	N	.	.	F	.	.	N	.	.	F

Note : Date is calculated with respect to the first i-band measurements. Band shows the band observed. Moon indicates whether the moon is full (F) or new (N). The columns are spaced by five days.

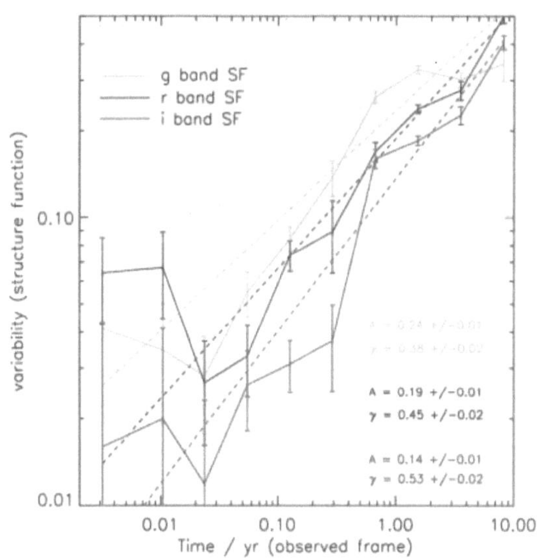

Variability structure functions (solid lines) for SDSS J203817.37+003029.8, based on the photometry for the g (green), r (blue) and i (red) band, computed from Equation. The best-fit power law) model for the structure function from the MCMC simulated annealing code are over-plotted as dashed lines. The corresponding A and γ parameters of the power law and their estimated errors are quoted in the lower right corner of the plot. Calculating similar structure functions by means of the power-law model for the 9157 Stripe 82 quasars

Power-Law Structure Functions for Sources in Stripe 82

Before doing so, we explore wether this power law behavior is present in an average sense. In Figure we show the median sample structure function, created by median-combining all the individual binned structure functions calculated with Equation separately for the well sampled Stripe 82 quasars (Section 2.4.1), F/G stars and RR Lyrae. The shaded regions in Figure around the medians enclose 68% and 95% of the individual structure functions. Figure shows that the quasar sample median of the binned structure function closely resembles a power law with $A = 0.093 \pm 0.0002$ and $\gamma = 0.43 \pm 0.002$, in agreement with findings elsewhere in the literature . In particular, a value of the slope of the sample median structure function of $\gamma = 0.43$ agrees well with most of the literature for a brief overview). Rough estimates of the 1-year observed frame power law amplitudes in the literature give amplitudes between 0.10 and 0.14 (depending on the assumed mean redshift of the samples), in good agreement with our estimate for A of 0.093 mag.

the sample structure functions of contaminants are also well described by power laws, but with small values of γ (i.e., they show no long-term growth in their variability). Note that the F/G stars, chosen to be non-variable, have a variability amplitude of ~0.04 mag. The RR Lyrae variability, when sparsely and randomly sampled in Stripe 82, looks like white noise ($|\gamma|$ 1) with an amplitude ~0.2 mag. Thus, the use of a power-law model of the form given in Equation seems to be a fairly good assumption, and different types of objects may differ both in amplitude and in slope of their structure function.

The power law fits to the three (binned) structure functions are shown as dashed lines. The A and γ with their estimated errors are given in the lower right corner of the plot.

Results

Having defined different sub-samples of sources, and having shown that we can sensibly quantify their light curve characteristics by a power-law structure function model, we now proceed to characterize each of these sources by their best-fit parameters A and γ. As opposed to the earlier SDSS analysis the improved time sampling of the Stripe 82 (and even Pan-STARRS 1) surveys, enables us to investigate the distributions of the A and γ parameters for the individual sources, not only for ensembles.

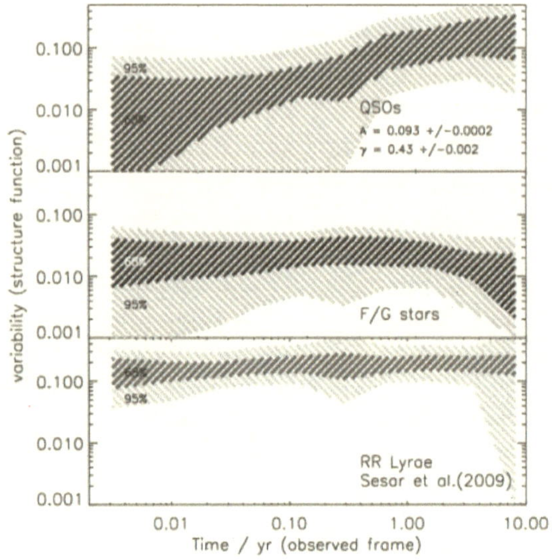

The sample-median r-band binned structure function for the quasars (top), F/G stars (center) and 483 RR Lyrae (bottom) in Stripe 82, calculated using Equation (2.7). The power-law nature of the three samples is clearly seen, by the approximate straight lines the structure functions trace. The power law parameters A and γ obtained by fitting the quasar sample structure function with the 2 parameter power law model in Equation are shown in the top panel. The shaded regions around each structure function indicate the 68% and 95% scatter around the median value.

The A–γ Distribution

The distribution of the variability characteristics, quantified by the bestfit A and γ for all the spectroscopically confirmed quasars, and for the 'contaminant' F/G stars and RR Lyrae, as described, based on their r-band Stripe 82 light curves. The histograms along the axes of the two-dimensional scatter plot show the projected parameter distribution of the quasars and of the contaminants. Inspection of Figure alone shows how well the spectroscopically confirmed quasars separate from the (stellar locus) contaminants in this space, demonstrating that the power-law structure function fit from a single band is an efficient classifier for data of this quality (~60 epochs). The analogous A–γ distributions for the much sparser Pan-STARRS 1-like sampling of the r-band measurements are shown in Figure : these parameter estimates are based on only 6 epochs of photometry over 3 years, rather than the ~60 in the full Stripe 82 survey. The separation of the quasars and the contaminants is less clean with the Pan-STARRS 1 sampling, but one nevertheless clearly sees a quasar-dominated region with rather low contamination. Plots analogous to the ones shown in Figures, but for the g, i and z-band measurements, show that on average A decreases by 30-50% going from g to z band, whereas γ is unchanged with varying wavelength. Thus, the separation of the quasars from the contaminants via their γ values appears to work comparably well in all 4 bands (with somewhat more scatter in the z-band). In agreement with Kozłowski et al. (2010), no clear difference in the ratio of the amplitudes at different wavelengths between RR Lyrae and quasars is detected.

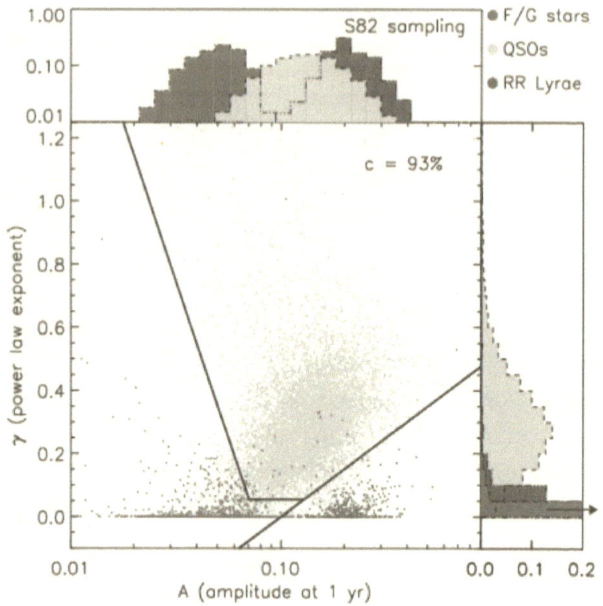

Distribution of the variability structure function parameters A and γ (Equation (2.8)) for ~15,000 individual objects in Stripe 82. The spectroscopically confirmed quasars are shown as light blue points; confirmed RR Lyrae and color-selected F/G stars are shown in red and grey, respectively. A separation of the quasars from the stellar locus contaminants is clearly seen. The three solid lines define the region in which we estimate the quasar completeness c of our algorithm (which turns out to be 93% in this case). Along the axes we show the projected A and γ distributions for the sub-samples.

Since most F/G stars should not vary, but RR Lyrae do, they should have different A distributions. This is seen in Figure 2.6 and 2.7: RR Lyrae have magnitude amplitudes above ~0.1, while the F/G stars have characteristic values of A ~ 0.01. It is therefore clear that our approach can also separate RR Lyrae from stellar (non-varying) contaminants without doing a full fit of a periodic light curve.

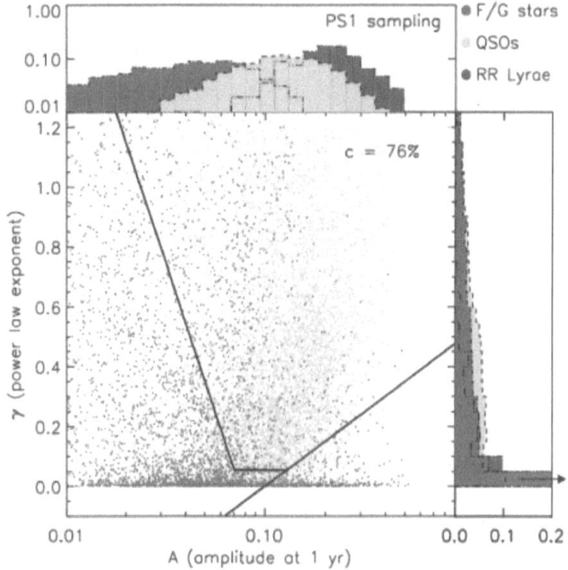

Distribution of the variability structure function parameters, similar, but after down-sampling to the 6 epochs Pan-STARRS 1 3π survey cadence. A variability separation of quasars and their contaminants is again apparent, albeit not as clearly as in Figure. The selection region is the same; the completeness is given in the upper right corner of the plot

Completeness and Purity

To move beyond a merely qualitative assessment of the separability of the quasars from contaminants we now estimate the achievable completeness and purity of the resulting sample. Purity is the more difficult quantity to estimate as it requires appropriate abundances for the contaminants. We do not have these for the training set quasar, F/G star and RR Lyrae samples, where the ratio of quasars to contaminants is 2:1, instead of a more realistic ~1:25, and we can therefore only estimate completeness when working with these samples. However, by design the UVX, nUVX and griz selection boxes give parent samples with the correct quasar-contaminants ratio: we use these to explore the purity of our quasar selection algorithm For the present we divide the A–γ plane by simple cuts that define a quasar selection box, and then quantify its performance. Specifically, our fiducial quasar selection region is bounded by the following three straight lines:

$$\begin{aligned}\gamma(A) &= 0.5 * \log(A) + 0.50 \\ \gamma(A) &= -2 * \log(A) - 2.25 \\ \gamma(A) &= 0.055 \,.\end{aligned}$$

This can be thought of as a way of providing lower limits on the available completeness and purity, that a more sophisticated selection procedure would improve upon. One could of course tweak the cuts in
previous Equations to explore the trade-off between purity and completeness, which we have only done here 'by eye.' Applying these cuts to the data leads to the completeness given in Table for the 'QSO+contam' catalog. The completeness is calculated as the fraction of spectroscopically confirmed quasars in the sample that fall within the cuts. In our simple illustrative setup we have a completeness of 93% for the quasars in the case where the time sampling is equal to Stripe 82 (~60 epochs). In the case of a Pan-STARRS 1-like time sampling the completeness drops to 76%.

Parent Cat.	Sampling	c	δc	p	δp	Quasar Reference Cat.
QSO+cont.	Stripe 82	93%	1%	-	-	SDSS
QSO+cont.	Pan-STARRS 1	76%	1%	-	-	SDSS
UVX	Stripe 82	90%	3%	95%	3%	SDSS+2SLAQ
UVX	Pan-STARRS 1	73%	2%	92%	3%	SDSS+2SLAQ
nUVX	Stripe 82	90%	15%	96%	16%	Visual
nUVX	Pan-STARRS 1	65%	12%	32%	5%	Visual
griz box	Stripe 82	92%	6%	92%	6%	Visual & SDSS+2SLAQ
griz box	Pan-STARRS 1	75%	6%	30%	2%	Visual & SDSS+2SLAQ

Of the RR Lyrae 97% and 83% (for the Stripe 82 and Pan-STARRS 1 sampling respectively) fall in the high-A low-γ corner below the line given by Equation. In this region 4, we were not able to investigate this decreased completeness further.

Quasars in the UVX catalog

For the UVX object sample there is enough spectroscopy in Stripe 82 to define a spectroscopically confirmed quasar subsample, a reference catalog of quasars which is complete in Stripe 82. By combining the spectroscopically confirmed quasars in Stripe 82, with the objects from the 2SLAQ (2-degree field SDSS luminous red galaxies and QSO) survey (Croom et al. 2009b), our final quasar reference catalog contains 11216 individual quasars (9157 from SDSS and 2059 from 2SLAQ). We only selected objects flagged as 'QSO' in the publicly available 2SLAQ data.1 Matching this quasar reference catalog with the catalog of UVX Stripe 82 point sources returned 2140 quasars out of the 2912 objects in the UVX catalog. Thus, 73% percent of the point sources in the UVX color box are known quasars. It is not surprising that the fraction is so large, since we used the powerful u – g color in the definition of the color box. This simply re-affirms that the UVX box is a region of color space where the quasars are in the majority, as they are well separated from the stellar locus by the u – g color; it is exactly this separation we are trying to find an alternative to. We estimated A and γ for the entire UVX catalog, using both the full (Stripe 82) sampling and the sparser Pan-STARRS 1-like version of it. The result is shown in the top row of the A–γ plots in Figure. Applying our simple variability selection cuts (Equations) returned 2033 and 1734 quasar candidates for the Stripe 82 and Pan-STARRS 1 sampling, respectively. Matching these objects with the 2140 know SDSS+2SLAQ quasars in the UVX catalog returned 1935 and 1573 matches. Thus we are able to detect the UVX quasars with a completeness of 90% and a purity of 95% (1935 matches/2033 candidates) when using the Stripe 82 time sampled data. For the Pan-STARRS 1-like sampling of the data we get a completeness of 73% and a purity of 92% (Table)

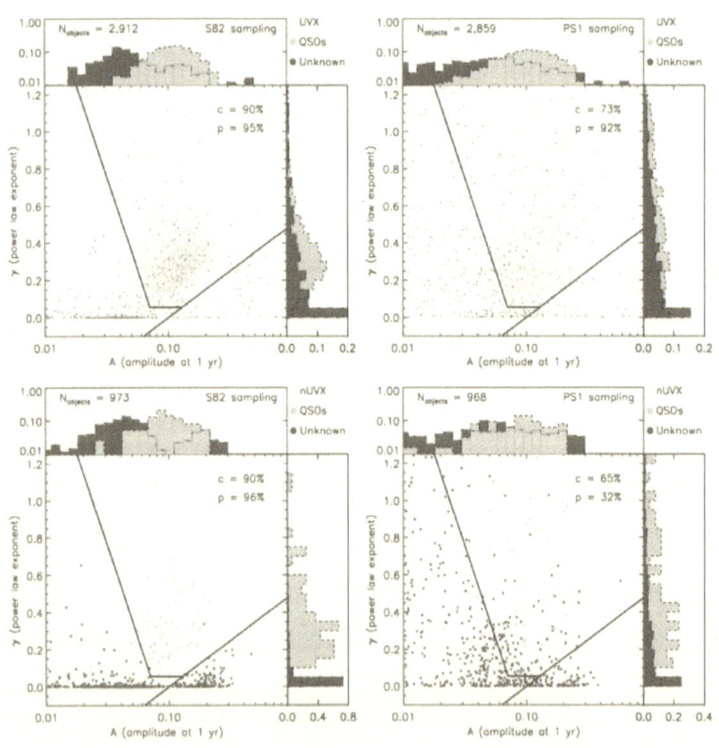

: Distribution of variability structure function power law parameters A and γ measured for the objects in the UVX and nUVX catalogs of Table. The left plots corresponds to the catalogs with a Stripe 82 time sampling, while the right plots correspond to the sparser PanSTARRS 1 time sampling (6 epochs over 3 years). The three solid lines in each scatter plot correspond to the quasar variability selection region defined by Equations. The completeness and purity estimates are shown in the upper right corner of each scatter plot, and in Table. In the upper left corner the total number of objects in the catalog is stated. The light blue points indicate the known quasars, and the red points all other objects. Along the axes of the two-dimensional scatter plots the projected probability distributions for A and γ are shown as histograms.

Quasars in the nUVX catalog

The catalog of the UVX point sources was deliberately chosen from a region of color space where the color selection already does a superb job finding quasars, as confirmed by the complete SDSS and 2SLAQ quasar catalog and the completeness and purity of our A–γ approach. However, one might argue that in this case (of UVX quasars) a light curve analysis adds little. To explore the A–γ approach further we applied it to the nonUV excess objects described. In the nUVX color box (Table) there is no simple way to quantify the completeness of the parent sample of color-selected objects, since we do not know how many quasars were missed in this region of color space during the SDSS survey. To try to quantify this, we extracted the spectra from the 973 objects in this catalog that were targeted for SDSS spectroscopy. By visually inspecting these spectra we were able to compile a catalog of 77 quasars among the Stripe 82 nUVX objects. (Of these 77, 6 quasars are not in the SDSS+2SLAQ catalog). This means that if the SDSS fibers had been allocated to nUVX objects randomly, then the purity of the nUVX quasar sample would be 77/973 = 8%. However, in practice the fibers were placed according to a Bayesian ranking that made fuller use of the color information, so that this 8% is likely an upper limit on the purity of the nUVX quasar sample. (The fraction of quasars hidden in the un-targeted nUVX objects is likely lower than the fraction of quasars found in the nUVX objects with spectra.)

Applying our A–γ analysis and our variability selection criteria to the spectroscopic subcatalog of 973 nUVX objects returned 72 (178) quasar candidates for the Stripe 82 (PanSTARRS 1-like) time sampling. The nUVX objects' variability parameters are plotted in the bottom row of Figure. Estimating the completeness and purity in the Stripe 82 sampling case, assuming that the 973 objects with spectra are a random subset of all the nUVX objects, gives that we are 90% complete and 96% pure (Table). By the same argument as above, the purity is an upper limit on the overall purity of the nUVX quasar sample whereas the completeness is exact. The purity and the completeness stand on their own in quantifying our ability to recover the spectroscopically confirmed quasars. Thus, the addition of the variability information enhances the purity to 96% instead of 8%, as is the case for the purely color-selected sample. In the case of the sparser PanSTARRS 1-like sampling we still have a completeness of 65%, and a purity of 32%. This clearly demonstrates that a variability-based approach is very efficient at selecting nUVX quasars when the data is well sampled in time. Even with the sparse Pan-STARRS 1 sampling, the purity increases by a factor of 4 when variability information is used.

The plot of the Stripe 82-sampled nUVX objects (lower left corner) shows a clear bimodality of the A parameter distribution of the unknown (red) objects. As seen with the object training set, this bimodality is a probable separation between the non-varying contaminants and the varying (possible RR Lyrae) contaminants. Thus the nUVX objects have been separated into quasar candidates (high γ; intermediate A), RR Lyrae candidates (low γ; high A) and non-varying stars (low γ; low A).

Quasars in the griz Color Box

To simulate quasar candidate selection without u-band photometry, we applied our variability analysis to the objects lying in a fairly large multi-color region in griz space, the so-called griz box defined. This color box fully contains an important part of the stellar locus. Estimating the completeness and purity of our algorithm for the griz box is difficult, as no clear estimates of the abundance of quasars exist for such a color cut. We therefore checked the quasar candidates against a catalog of the SDSS+2SLAQ quasars, plus the 6 extra quasars found via the visual inspection of the nUVX spectra. This may fall considerably short of a complete sample of quasars, but at the moment it is the best we can do; the purities calculated in this section are therefore lower limits. Matching this quasar reference catalog to the 12,714 objects in the griz box we found 443 known quasars. Estimating A–γ for all these sources, returned 442 (1,118) variability-based quasar candidates, when considering the Stripe 82 (PanSTARRS 1) sampling and when applying the A–γ cuts of Equations. Of these candidates 407 (333) were found to be known quasars. Thus, for the broad griz color pre-selection, variability selection achieves 92%(75%) completeness and a purity of 92%(30%) for the Stripe 82 (Pan-STARRS 1) sampled data, respectively. The A and γ distributions for the griz box selected objects are shown in the top panel (Stripe 82 sampling) and 2.10 (Pan-STARRS 1 sampling).

We have projected our variability selected quasar candidates back into ugr and gri color space, in order to understand the color distributions of variability selected quasar candidates. The figures show that 86% and 98% of the not spectroscopically confirmed candidates fall on the gri stellar locus, defined as the (blue) contour level containing 95% of the stellar locus objects in Stripe 82. This suggests that many, if not most, of these unconfirmed quasar candidates are stars scattered into our variability selection region. However, there are some possible quasars among the unknowns judging from their colors. For instance, a few of the unknown objects (6% and 1% in the Stripe 82 and Pan-STARRS 1 sampled case respectively) fall in the ugr UVX selection box. This illustrates that our purity estimates are lower limits but close to the likely truth. It also shows that the ugriz quasar color selection in SDSS (Richards et al. 2002b, 2006, 2009) has done an excellent job, implying that < 10% of the quasars with i < 19.1 are 'hiding' in the stellar locus and have been missed by the SDSS selection.

When defining the griz box. We included the stellar locus to achieve as high a completeness as possible and to illustrate the prospects of our approach. However, removing objects falling within the stellar locus, could greatly enhance the purity at a modest reduction of the completeness. Thus, selecting quasar candidates without u-band information can be put into four scenarios:

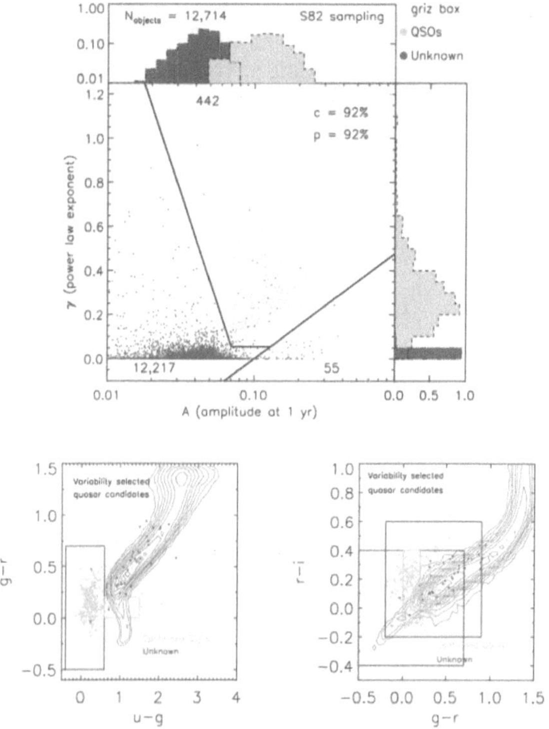

The top panel shows the A and γ power law parameter space of the objects in the griz selection box with Stripe 82 time sampling. The projected probability distributions for A and γ for the confirmed quasars (light blue points) and the unknown objects (red points) are shown as histograms. The solid lines indicate the selection cut defined in Equations. The numbers 12,217, 442 and 55 in the A–γ plane indicate the number of objects in the given region. The estimated completeness and purity is shown in the upper right corner of the scatter plot. The bottom row shows the 442 variability selected quasar candidates (407 confirmed quasars and 35 unknown candidates) from the A–γ space, projected back into ugr and gri color space. The black, green and blue boxes correspond to the UVX, nUVX and griz selection boxes . 87% of the confirmed quasars and 6% of the unknown candidates fall in the black UVX box in ugr color space (lower left plot). 5% and 6% of the quasars and unknowns fall in the green nUVX box. The contours in the bottom plots indicate the Stripe 82 stellar locus. 95% of the stellar locus objects are within the blue contour level (the last but one outer contour). Above 80% of the 35 unknown candidates and 41% of the 407 confirmed quasars fall within the blue gri contour, providing an estimate of the number of quasars 'hiding' in the gri stellar locus.

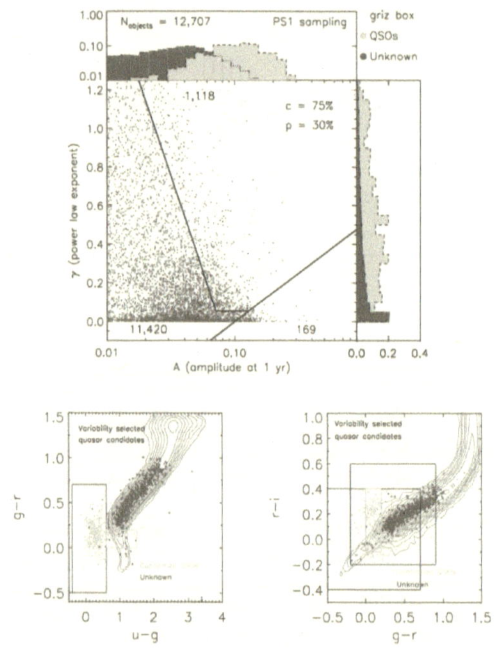

Plots similar to those for the griz selection box data down-sampled to a Pan-STARRS 1 cadence (6 epochs over 3 years). The numbers 11,420, 1,118 and 169 in A–γ space (top panel) indicate the number of objects in each of the three regions defined by the black solid lines as defined in Equations. The estimated completeness and purity of the 1,118 variability selected quasar candidates is shown in the upper right corner of the top panel. Of these 1,118 objects, 42% of the confirmed quasars and 98% of the unknown candidates fall within the blue gri color space (lower right plot) stellar locus contour level, which encloses 95% of the Stripe 82 stellar locus objects. 87% of the confirmed quasars fall in the black UVX selection box in ugr color space (lower left plot), as opposed to only 1% of the unknowns. In the green ugr nUVX box fall 5% and 1% of the quasars and unknown candidates. These percentages indicate that most of the unknowns are stars scattered into our selection region due to the 6 epoch sampling of Pan-STARRS 1.

1) A 'naive' griz box (i < 19.1) including the stellar locus and not considering variability information will have a quasar selection completeness above 90%, but a purity of only 4%.

2) Taking a griz box color selection, but cutting out the stellar locus (defined by the (blue) contour in Figures 2.9 and 2.10) and still not considering variability information improves the purity to ~48% but lowers the completeness to ~59%. This is what would be easily achievable in a single-epoch griz survey.

3) Combining a griz color selection including the stellar locus, but considering variability information leads to a completeness of 92%(75%) and a purity of 92%(30%) for the Stripe 82 (Pan-STARRS 1) sampled data, respectively. This means that Pan-STARRS 1 can provide a 75% complete quasar sample, if 30% purity were acceptable.

4) Finally, removing the stellar locus from the griz selection box and combining this with variability information lowers the completeness to 54%(44%), but returns a purity of 97%(92%) with Stripe 82 (Pan-STARRS 1) time-sampled data. PanSTARRS 1 can provide a high purity quasar sample that is ~50% complete.

This illustrates how a variability selection cut greatly improves the candidate sample as compared to quasar candidate selection based on colors alone when u-band information is not available.

Keeping in mind that the purities calculated here are lower limits, these results suggest that the variability selection of quasar candidates in Pan-STARRS 1 or other multi-epoch surveys will produce high quality, extensive samples.

Probabilistic Combination of Selection Methods

With surveys like Pan-STARRS others, large amounts of data will become available in the (near) future. The science become more feasible with quasar catalogs containing more than a million actual quasars, however, new methods for selecting quasars will also be needed to avoid spectroscopic follow-up confirmation, which becomes unfeasible with such large quasar (candidate) samples. One of these new selection methods could very well be the intrinsic variability of quasars as presented here. That being said, only relying on one method for detecting quasars is far from the optimal. Therefore, a main focus of the quasar selection community should be to combine existing, and possibly new, selection methods for quasars. As argued, quasars are extremely versatile, so the work put into such an effort will definitely pay off.

The above text has mostly focused on the selection of quasars via a structure function parameterization of variability and the standard SDSS ugriz color selection. However, these are (obviously) not the only methods proposed for selecting quasars in the literature. For instance, it is not only in the optical bands that quasars can be selected convincingly based on their colors. Also near-infrared colors have been shown to aid quasar selection. After the results presented in this chapter were published in Schmidt et al. (2010) also several other methods using the intrinsic variability of quasars as a selection tool have been proposed. In MacLeod et al. (2010, 2011); Kozłowski et al. (2010) and Butler & Bloom (2011) they base their color selection on the modeling of quasar light curves as a damped random walk, as presented in Kelly et al. (2009, 2010), by parametrizing the variability by the characteristic damping time-scale, τ, and the asymptotic magnitude of a structure function, SF∞. In Palanque-Delabrouille et al. (2011) they base a neural network scheme on the A–γ selection presented in this chapter, and in Kim et al. (2011) a selection method using support vector machines on extracted parameters such as period, variability amplitude, and color, was used to select quasar candidates. Hence, quasar variability selection presently offers several (partially correlated) selection parameters.

Combining all the methods based on colors as well as variability would without a doubt strengthen the selection of quasars. One could imagine representing each of the different selection methods and selection parameters in a probabilistic way, such that they can easily be combined to a 'unified selection' of quasars. A scheme where the overall 'grand' probability, P, of a given object being a quasar is given by something like

$$\mathscr{P}_{\rm QSO} = \frac{1}{N_{\rm methods}} \prod_{i}^{N_{\rm methods}} w_i \, {\rm P}_i \ ,$$

with i counting the different selection methods, e.g., (A, γ), (u – g, g – r), (J – K, i – Y), (SF∞, τ), (period,amplitude), etc., Pi giving the probability that the object is a quasar according to method i, and wi representing some clever weighting, would accomplish that. The weighting scheme should be created such that cases where a given selection method does not provide a sensible Pi due to for instance lack of epochs (variability) or wavelength coverage (colors), are taken probably into account. How to actually do this in practice is still not clear, but attempts at creating probabilistic selection schemes (so far only based on colors) have been presented (Mortlock et al. 2011a; Kirkpatrick et al. 2011; Bovy et al. 2011).

An example of how combining different selection methods improves the final results is also presented in Wu et al. (2011) (though not in a probabilistic manor like proposed above). Our goal with this study was to find the 'missing' quasars at z ~ 2.7 mentioned in combining the variability selection presented in this chapter with the optical/near-infrared color selection presented in (Wu & Jia 2010). The spectroscopic follow-up of our final candidate sample revealed a 100% success-rate, which speaks for itself and nicely illustrates the power of combining quasar selection methods.

Selecting Lensed Quasars with Variability

With new and larger quasar samples another very interesting prospect of the work presented here is the possibility of finding lensed quasars. As mentioned gravitational lenses, and in particular gravitationally lensed quasars, have a wide range of applications. For instance, the anomalous brightnesses of quasar lenses probe the small scale dark matter content of (the lens) galaxies, microlensing of the images by stars in the lens galaxies allows the central AGN

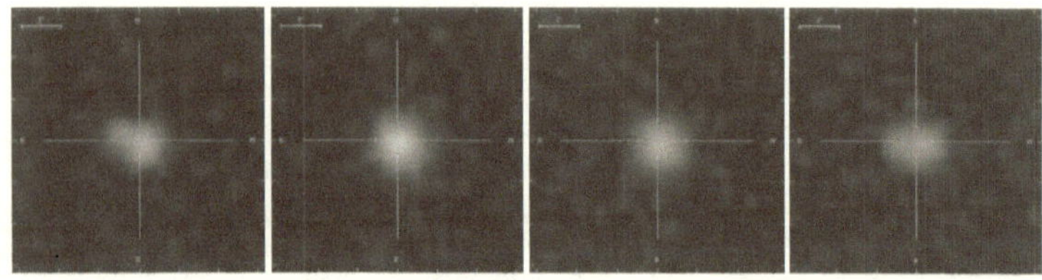

SDSS thumbnails (approximately 12×12 arcsec) of four high priority smallseparation quasar lens candidates selected via intrinsic quasar variability as described in this chapter. Confirming any of these as an actual lens will be the first time a lens has been found via variability and will serve as the proof-of-concept for dedicated variability lens searches on large areas of the sky, e.g., the 3π survey of Pan-STARRS 1.

region of the quasars to be super-resolved and the lens magnification enables the host galaxy to be studied, i.e., it becomes possible to study the scaling relations between the quasar host and the central black holes. At present only ~100 lensed quasar systems are known, and for any given lensing application only a small fraction of these is suitable. Hence, enhancing the number of known quasar lenses will enable a more detailed exploration of many of the applications mentioned above.

In the work presented here, we have mainly focused on point source selection, with the purpose of finding quasar candidates. Such an approach would be directly applicable to a search for wide separation lenses, where (by definition) the multiple images are well-resolved. With the overwhelming sample sizes of the upcoming quasar catalogs the number of wide separation lensed quasars occurring as multiple quasar detection within a relatively small projected distance on the sky will be significant. It will be a relatively straight forward exercise to search the new quasar catalogs, for instance created with a probabilistic 'unified selection' as the one described above, for close pairs of quasars. There is a high chance that such pairs turn out to be multiple images of the same quasar, i.e., a lens. In the cases where they turn out to be at different redshifts, these quasar constellations are still valuable and have several interesting applications.

But also small-separation quasar lenses can potentially be identified through their variability. As these are unresolved for optical intermediate resolution surveys like SDSS, applying for example the A–γ variability selection algorithm presented here to spatially extended (rather than point sources), yet quasar-colored, objects will return a list of small separation quasar lens candidates.

We have initiated such a search on SDSS Stripe 82 with promising preliminary results. By selecting objects with quasar colors, extended morphologies, quasar variability according to A and γ, and suitable photometric (or spectroscopic when available) redshift to be a lens, we have collected a sample of a few hundred small-separation lens candidates. In Figure 4 of the highest priority lens candidates are shown. We expect that of the order 10 of these candidates are indeed lenses. We have initiated a high resolution photometric follow-up program (either in near-infrared or with space based observatories) in an attempt to resolve the lens-components and possibly the lens galaxy. So far we have obtained La Silla 2.2 m GROND near-infrared photometry for around 40 of our candidates, but have not yet analyzed the data. Furthermore, a proposal for HST followup of some of the highest ranked candidates has recently been submitted. In cases where the photometric follow-up reveals particularly interesting (now hopefully resolved) candidates, a second spectroscopic follow-up is most probably needed to confirm the lens nature of the candidate. If a candidate is confirmed as a lens, this will be the first time a gravitational lens has been found based on the intrinsic variability of the source.

This pilot study, which we plan to present in a forthcoming paper, will therefore be a proof-of-concept for selecting lenses with variability and a first step in effectuating such a search on larger areas of the sky with multi-epoch data, e.g., the 3π (3/4 of the sky) area of the Pan-STARRS 1 survey, where as many as 2000 lenses are expected (Oguri & Marshall 2010).

CHAPTER THREE

The Quasar Color Variability

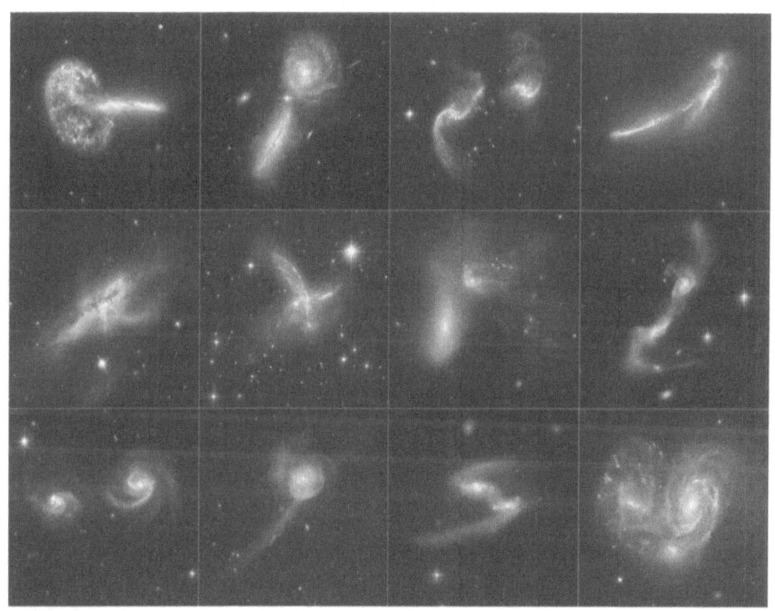

In this chapter we quantify quasar color variability using the quasar variability database from Chapter 2, i.e., ugriz photometry of ~9000 quasars from SDSS Stripe 82, observed over ~8 years at ~60 epochs each. We confirm previous reports that quasars become bluer when brightening. We find a redshift dependence of this blueing in a given set of bands (e.g., g and r), but show that it is the result of the flux contribution from less variable or delayed emission lines in the different SDSS bands at different redshifts. After correcting for this effect, quasar color variability is remarkably uniform, and independent not only of redshift, but also of quasar luminosity and black hole mass. The color variations of individual quasars, as they vary in brightness on year timescales, are much more pronounced than the ranges in color seen in samples of quasars across many orders of magnitude in luminosity. This indicates distinct physical mechanisms behind quasar variability and the observed range of quasar luminosities at a given black hole mass – quasar variations cannot be explained by changes in the mean accretion rate. We do find some dependence of the color variability on the characteristics of the flux variations themselves, with fast, low-amplitude, brightness variations producing more color variability. The observed behavior could arise if quasar variability results from flares or ephemeral hot spots in an accretion disk.

Probing the Physics of Quasars

The generally accepted model of AGN described has several observational features that makes it possible to probe and extract information about the physics governing this spectacular galaxy evolution phase. The three main observables of AGN and quasars that provide information about the underlying physics are: photometry over most of the electromagnetic spectrum from hard x-rays to radio, the quasar spectra and their broad as well as narrow emission lines and the variability (probably) produced by the accretion disk nature of the AGN, which we used as a selection tool to find quasar candidates. In this section we will present some of the methods used to probe the physics and characteristics of quasars and their central engine, before we in the reminder of this chapter describe a new study that combines the spectral features and the variability to gain new general knowledge about AGN.

The (Rest-Frame Optical) Quasar Spectrum

The electromagnetic spectrum is one of the main providers of precise and detailed information about the physics of AGN and quasars in particular, but of all astronomical objects in general – it is popularly said that photometry and imaging is astronomy, whereas spectroscopy is astrophysics; which is not without a good reason. This will also become evident in the following subsections where many of them are closely linked to the information the quasar spectrum provides.

We show the composite quasar spectrum of Vanden Berk et al. (2001). The quasar spectrum represents the spectra of the general population of AGN (see Table) and consists of four main components: (i) the absorption blueward of the Lyα emission, (ii) the power-law continuum, (iii) the broad emission lines and (iv) the narrow emission lines.

The pronounced absorption at wavelengths shorter than the Lyα emission at 1216 Å is produced by absorption from intervening columns of neutral hydrogen (Hi) in the quasar line of sight, and is present in all distant quasars and AGN as well as 'normal' galaxies. Photons of energy 10.2 eV (corresponding to λ =1216 Å) can excite the neutral hydrogen from its ground state and hence be absorbed. Due to the redshifting of light, caused by the expansion of the Universe while traveling from the distant quasar to the observer, the energy of photons is diluted, i.e., the wavelength becomes longer/redder. This means that at some point all wavelengths initially more energetic than 10.2 eV in the quasar spectrum, i.e., blueward of Lyα will have been diluted to 10.2 eV so it can be absorbed by any neutral hydrogen it might encounter. Hence, the Lyα absorption lines fill up basically all wavelengths blueward of the Lyα emission (which comes from the quasar itself) like 'trees' in a forest, and is therefore also referred to as the Lyα forest. The density of the hydrogen the photons encounter determines the amount of absorption, such that very dense regions in the line of sight, e.g., galaxies, will strongly absorb the light and give rise to pronounced broad absorption features. These systems are referred to as damped Lyα systems or Lyman limit systems. The Lyα forest therefore maps the hydrogen column densities in the line of sight to the quasar, which for quasars at high redshift, corresponds to a significant fraction of the Hubble volume. This has been used for several studies both mapping individual galaxies and the intergalactic medium. For further details on the Lyα forest and its applications.

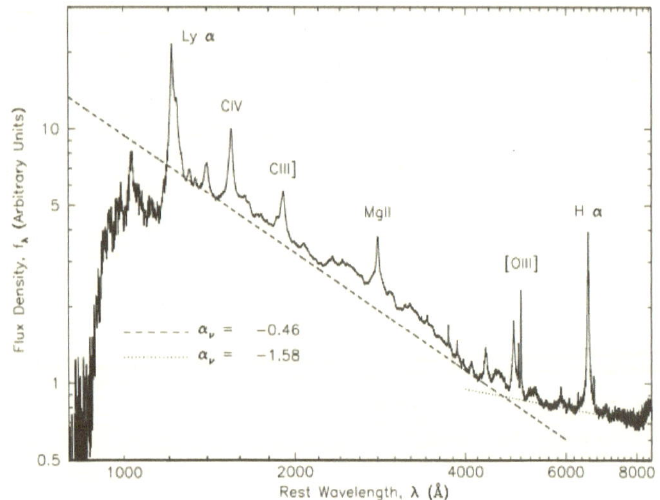

Composite quasar spectrum showing the main features of most AGN spectra: the absorption bluewards of Lyα referred to as the Lyα forest, the broken power-law non-thermal continuum, and the broad and narrow emission lines. For a more detailed version of the spectrum.

The second important feature of the quasar spectrum is the power-law continuum, which as illustrated in Figure and described in for instance, is actually best approximated by a broken power-law in the rest-frame optical spectral range. The quasar continuum arrises from the radiating accretion disk of the AGN, i.e., it is not the sum of billions of blackbody radiating stars as the spectra of normal galaxies basically are, and is therefore non-thermal. However, the break in the power-law slope, also referred to as the 'near-infrared inflection', is presumably caused by emission from hot dust and an increased significance of the underlying host-galaxy (stellar blackbody) light (Vanden Berk et al. 2001). Attempts at reproducing this particular quasar continuum shape in models has provided many constraints and large insight into the physics of the central engine. This is very well illustrated by the lengthy discussion of the AGN accretion disk continuum spectrum in for instance Krolik (1999). The clear distinction between the spectra of standard black-body stars (and hence galaxies) is what makes the color selection of quasars described so efficient.

The last prominent features of any quasar spectrum are the broad and narrow emission lines. These are produced in the broad and narrow line regions (BLR and NLR) described and illustrated in Figure. Several processes contribute to the line emission in AGN, for example the narrow lines might have a significant contribution from the narrow lines of the host galaxy (stellar) spectrum. However, by far the most important process is photoionization of the BLR and NLR clouds by the nonthermal continuum radiation of the accretion disk. The emission lines are thought to be absorption of high energy photons which are then re-emitted at the characteristic wavelengths of the atomic electron-levels. The width of the individual lines are determined by the Doppler-broadening arising from the kinematics of the BLR and NLR clouds. 'Broad' lines are usually defined as lines with widths $\sigma v > 1000$ km/s, whereas narrow lines usually have $\sigma v \sim 100$ km/s, as also noted in Table. Quasar and AGN emission lines have proven very useful for gaining information about quasar physics as the following subsections will show. For a detailed description of AGN emission lines see Krolik (1999) and Vanden Berk et al. (2001).

Eddington Ratios and Black Hole Masses

Two of the main parameters used in the literature to describe AGN is the mass of the central black hole and the Eddington ratio. The mass of the central black hole is often obtained by inferring the velocity of the BLR (vBLR) from measurements of the velocity broadening of the broad emission lines (σvBLR) in the AGN spectrum, and combining that with simple assumptions about the characteristic size of the BLR (rBLR; or obtained from reverberation mapping as described below) such that

$$M_{\rm vir} \propto \frac{r_{\rm BLR} v_{\rm BLR}^2}{G} \quad .$$

To be specific, what is actually obtained is the virial mass enclosed by the BLR clouds, which is assumed to approximate the actual mass of the central black hole, MBH. This is done under the assumption that the gravity (and not radiation pressure or magnetic fields) dominates the velocity broadening of the emission lines. Corrections of this assumption have been discussed (e.g., Peterson 2010).

With an estimate of the central black hole mass, the Eddington Luminosity is easily obtained via Equation , and from that the Eddington ratio, which is defined as the ratio between the bolometric luminosity of the AGN and the Eddington Luminosity, i.e., (Lbol/LEdd). The Eddington ratio is also calculated under certain assumptions. Since its definition requires an estimate of the bolometric luminosity, i.e., the luminosity corresponding to the integrated flux of the full AGN spectral energy distribution, a bolometric correction is assumed to link observable luminosities to the bolometric luminosity. The Eddington ratio indicates the accretion state of the AGN, as it relates to actual luminosity of the object to the theoretically determined Eddington accretion limit.

Several catalogs of AGN and quasar samples with these two key parameters have been published and discussed in the literature.

Emission Line Ratio Diagnostic – The BPT Diagram

Not only do the (broad) emission lines of quasars and AGN provide information about the physics of their hosts, they can also help distinguishing AGN from 'normal' emission line galaxies, and have been used to divide the AGN population into individual subpopulations, as was also illustrated in Figure and becomes clear when inspecting Table. One of the preferred methods to make such a distinction is the so-called BPT diagram first presented in Baldwin et al. (1981). We show an example of such a classification scheme from Trouille et al. (2011). Here the line ratios of the prominent [Oiii] and Hα emission lines with respect to Hβ and [Nii] are plotted. These line ratios are a good proxy for the degree of ionization of the gas in the observed galaxy. The level of ionization reflects the ability of the radiation to actually strip the electrons from the atoms in the gas via photoionization, and since the quasar/ AGN spectrum has a much larger fraction of high-energy (low wavelength) photons than ordinary galaxies, i.e., AGN spectra are harder than normal galaxies', the BPT diagram, or 'line-ratio'-diagram, has proven very useful for distinguishing AGN from normal star-bursting galaxies as well as AGN diagnostics. The applicability of the BPT diagram is of course limited by the availability of the emission lines and has mostly been applied to low-redshift galaxies (from for instance SDSS) where the emission lines fall in the optical pass-bands. However, if the [Oiii]–Hβ and Hα–[Nii] emission line features can be followed into the near-infrared as the object redshift increases, the BPT diagram diagnostics can also be applied out to higher redshifts. This is in principle possible with for example the 3D-HST survey, though higher resolution follow-up is needed to obtain confident line ratios, as only [Oiii]–Hβ is (marginally) resolved in the 3D-HST spectra.

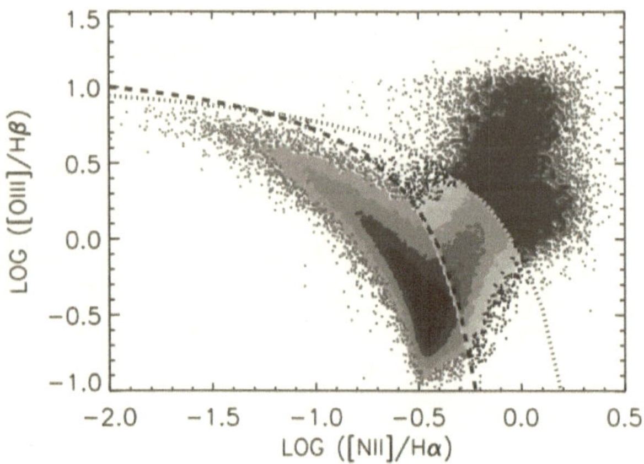

The BPT diagram. The plotted emission line ratios [Oiii]/Hβ and [Nii]/Hα are a good proxy for the level of ionization of the observed gas, and since AGN spectra are generally harder than 'normal' star-bursting emission line galaxies' spectra, the BPT diagram, i.e., the emission line ratios, serve as an excellent AGN classifier. The blue points are star-bursting galaxies, the gray point are composite galaxies, and the red points are AGN. The dashed and dotted lines separating these regions are defined in Kewley et al. (2001) and Kauffmann et al. (2003). With other line ratios the AGN cloud can be subdivided into different classes of AGN.

The Variability of Quasars

The different models of AGN variability mentioned have variability on many different timescales. From weeks for changes on thermal timescales in the accretion disk, over months for superpositions of stochastic processes, to several years for viscous changes in the large-scale structures of the accretion disk and for lens crossing times. These 'physical' timescales of AGN can be compared to the observed AGN variability timescales. The observed variability timescales span the range from a few hours, possibly the result of processes in a jet (Kelly et al. 2009), to months and years where quasars as mentioned are known to typically vary by & 10%. A longstanding challenge for any AGN theory is to disentangle these processes based on variability-timescales alone, and from that sort out which variability mechanisms are prevalent under what circumstance, and which mechanisms are responsible for which variations.

Moreover, AGN generally have power-law-shaped structure functions for the temporal variations, i.e., with no particular timescales, and because measurements of 'characteristic variability timescales' are likely dominated, or at least influenced by window functions, interpretations of variability time-scales are always somewhat problematic. All this being said, as described earlier, there seems to be a general consensus in the community, that the most probable scenario for the majority of the observed variability behavior is changes in the accretion disk.

The many observations of these intrinsic variability timescales of quasars and AGN provide a unique tool for probing the physics and the geometry of the central regions of the AGN; for instance via performing reverberation mapping.

Reverberation Mapping - Measuring Sizes of BLRs

Reverberation mapping deals with the monitoring of continuum variations in AGN, and the determination of how the emission lines react to that variation in form of an echo or reverberation, to constrain the geometry of the inner regions of the AGN. Blandford & McKee (1982) outlined the theoretical framework of reverberation mapping (and named it), but also noted that due to the variability timescales expected for a standard AGN, the observational challenges are many. Since 1982 many improvements have been made to the observational campaigns for reverberation mapping, which in 2010 had let to the precise measurements of the size of the BLR in ~45 AGN (Peterson 2010).

The goal of reverberation mapping is to constrain the so-called transfer function, which describes the BLR in velocity–time-lag (v, τ) space. Hence, the key observations are velocity of the individual BLR clouds, and the time-lag between the variations of the spectrum continuum and the emission lines. As mentioned above, part of the observed variability in AGN is of the order days to months. These requirements, i.e., finely sampled (days) observations over long periods of time (years), are what make spectroscopic reverberation mapping an observational challenge. If the data is available the structure of the BLR can be determined by assuming that the observed time delays are caused by light traveling times between the central continuum source and the BLR, implying that

$$r_{BLR} = c\,\tau\,.$$

This is the simplified version of the transfer function where the velocity is assumed to be the same for all BLR clouds. The size of the time-lag is therefore a proxy for the BLR size. We know from detailed reverberation mapping studies that τ can be of the order years for quasars at z ~ 1. This can be done for individual pairs of epochs of observations, and has let to the discovery of a strong correlation between rBLR and the luminosity L , with rBLR ∝ L 0.5 . This size-luminosity relation and the estimate of the BLR size are used to calibrate the single-epoch mass estimates obtained with Equation. Hence, with the benefit of the statistic of the many observation epochs in reverberation mapping campaigns, which give reliable (average) emission line widths, reverberation mapping provides reliable direct measurements of the black hole mass (via Equation) and the size of the BLR, as opposed to other more indirect estimates, such as scaling relations and AGN line widths.

To obtain the interplay between the continuum and emission lines, historically reverberation mapping has only been done by monitoring the AGN spectroscopically. However, the results presented in this chapter as well as the work by Haas et al. (2011) and Chelouche & Daniel (2012), illustrate the possibility of performing photometric reverberation mapping, making reverberation mapping of large samples of objects feasible, with the potential of improving the number of robustly measured BLR sizes and MBH by orders of magnitude.

Spectral Hardness – Brighter Means Blue

The last diagnostic of AGN and quasar physics we will describe in this short summary, and which will be a main topic of the rest of this chapter, is the characterization of the emitted spectrum described above and illustrated in Figure. Available multiwavelength AGN variability data provide clear, albeit somewhat qualitative, evidence that quasars tend to get bluer when they get brighter, i.e., the quasar spectrum gets harder with relatively more high-energy (blue) radiation. Whether this is a consequence of hardening of the variable spectrum, or because the variable blue component becomes more dominant compared to the non-variable red spectral component of the underlying host galaxy, is a matter of debate. This correlation between luminosity and spectral shape of the quasar provide information on the variability type, and can be used to further constrain AGN (variability) models.

One practical caveat to almost all the photometric 'brighter makes bluer' claims mentioned above, is that they are based on fitting in flux vs. color space, without accounting for the color-magnitude error correlation in the modeling. Such fitting may lead to spurious, or at least biased, results. To avoid these error correlations such analyses should be performed on flux-flux space. We will quantify this further below, as we in this chapter develop a better unbiased fitting procedure to quantify whether brighter-makes-bluer on short time-scales.

Furthermore, we will in the reminder of this chapter, carry out a comprehensive study of color variability in quasars, i.e., we study how flux variability is linked to changes of the (observed) optical colors. We provide both a detailed empirical description of the observed variability, and work on linking it to the physics of the quasar central engine, by quantifying the correlation of color variability with the redshift of the quasars, their MBH, Lbol/LEdd, and the temporal behavior of the flux variations. While the temporal behavior has been studied extensively, there are no comprehensive studies of color variability in large quasar samples with many epochs of data, which as described above, offers great potential as a diagnostic of accretion disk physics.

SDSS Stripe 82 Data

The Sloan Digital Sky Survey's (SDSS's) Stripe 82 is as mentioned an equatorial stripe 2.5 degrees wide and about 120 degrees long which has been observed many times in the 5 SDSS bands over more than 8 years. The Stripe 82 data base therefore provides an unprecedented collection of data for variability studies in general and quasars in particular. The analysis presented here is done on the ~9,000 spectroscopically confirmed quasars in Stripe 82. They have been selected from the SDSS data archive1 as described. Thus, we have a sample of quasars with on average 60 observations spread over a period of roughly 8 years. To obtain further information on each individual quasar, such as for instance estimates of the bolometric luminosity (Lbol) and black hole mass of the central engine (MBH), we crossmatched our list of objects with the catalog of quasar properties presented in Shen et al. (2011). We found a total of 9093 matches which constitute the catalog we will use in the remainder of this chapter, unless noted otherwise. This corresponds to basically the complete catalog of spectroscopically confirmed quasars in Stripe 82, hence, matching to the Shen et al. (2011) catalog did not cut down the sample much.

Fitting Color Variability in Magnitude Space

In principle optical color variability of quasars, i.e., the tendency of changing color, generally becoming bluer when they brighten, has been well established as described. However, as noted this color variability has been established and quantified by fitting data in color-magnitude space, for instance in g vs. (g – r) space, which suffers from co-variances between the color and the magnitude uncertainties that have not been accounted for in the past analyses. As we described, we have found that this may lead to severe overestimates of the color variability, especially as the photometric errors are not negligible compared to the intrinsic variability amplitudes. To remedy these biases we fit the color variability in magnitude-magnitude space, and then 'translate' them into color-magnitude relations.

The Stripe 82 data presented are unprecedented in their combination of time coverage, number of epochs, filter bands and sample size, which allows us to take the color variability analysis to the next level. Since the quasar variability typically shows modest amplitude (a few tenths of a magnitude or less) it has been characterized in previous work by a linear relation in flux-flux space. We make the ansatz that the photometric measurements of each individual quasar can be represented by a linear relation in gr-space (and ui-space). The gr and ui spaces were chosen for high signalto-noise and broad spectral range respectively (the uz-space being too uncertain due to z-band measurement errors). By calculating the Pearson correlation coefficient (PCC) for each individual quasar we verified that this approach is indeed sensible.

Averaged over the full sample in gr-space the PCC = 0.8. A PCC of 1 indicates a linear correlation with basically no scatter. Including an extra parameter in the linear relation to resemble the intrinsic scatter when determining sgr also shows that the scatter of the assumed linear relation is insignificant. Hence, the data do indeed resemble a linear relation quite closely. When fitting such data a number of factors need to be taken into account: there are comparable errors along both axes, e.g., for g and r magnitudes, the errors vary widely among different data points, and there are 'outliers'. In order to take these factors properly into account we have used the linear fitting approach, including outlier pruning, laid out in Hogg et al. (2010) In practice we identify the set of relations that make the data likely outcomes

$$r - \langle r \rangle = s'_{gr}(g - \langle g \rangle) + b$$

by a Metropolis-Hastings Markov chain Monte Carlo (MCMC) approach. Thus, we are determining the color variability (slope) s 0 gr and the offset on the r-axis b (moving each object to its mean g and r value to improve the determination of b) by sampling the parameter space via a MCMC chain. From simple algebraic manipulations of Equation we have that

$$\begin{aligned} r &= s'_{gr} g + b' \\ g - r &= -(s'_{gr} - 1)(g - \langle g \rangle) + B \, , \end{aligned}$$

where b 0 = hri − s 0 grhgi + b and B = −b + (hgi − hri) are constants. These equations give the 'transformation' of the fit between magnitude-magnitude space and color-magnitude space. If (s 0 gr – 1) < 0, i.e., if s 0 gr < 1 the quasar gets bluer as it brightens. In the remainder of this chapter we will use

$$s_{gr} = (s'_{gr} - 1)$$

as our definition of the color variability. In more general terms this corresponds to sλ1λ2 ≡ ∂mλ2 /∂mλ1 – 1 where the λs refer to the photometric bands. This expression has the intuitive

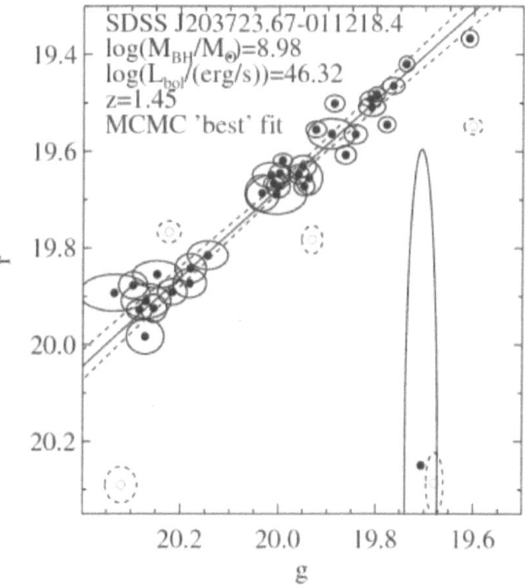

Example of MCMC fitting for the gr color variability, given a set of independently measured g and r light curve points and their uncertainties. These photometric data for the quasar SDSS J2037-0112 are shown as black circles with error ellipses indicating the photometric errors on the measurements. The solid blue line indicates the MCMC 'best' fit (i.e., the parameters for which the data are most likely) of the linear relation in Equation to the data that resulted from the MCMC chain, as described and in Hogg et al. (2010). The dashed blue lines show the 68% confidence interval of the MCMC. The empty data points with dashed error ellipses have a posterior probability of being outliers to the relation of > 50%, as described; see in Hogg et al. (2010). Note that the filled point in the lower right corner is not counted as an outlier, due to its large photometric error in r. This fitting accounts for the independence of the g and r measurements, the widely varying error bars, and the fact that even data as well-calibrated as SDSS Stripe 82 have 'outliers'. In the upper left corner we note the mass of the central black hole and the bolometric luminosity taken from the value-added quasar catalog presented in Shen et al. (2011), and the spectroscopic SDSS redshift of the object. In this manner the gr and ui color variability of each of the 9093 Stripe 82 quasars in the sample were determined.

interpretation that sgr = 0 means no color variability, i.e., brightness variation at constant color, whereas sgr < 0 accounts for the bluer equals brighter trend (the most common trend in the data) and sgr > 0 implies objects that become redder when they brighten.

In an example of such a MCMC fit to constrain the color variability is shown for the quasar SDSS J2037-0112 in gr space. The filled circles represent the individual photometric epochs from Stripe 82, with the ellipses indicating the photometric errors in g and r. The 'best' fit from Equation is shown as the blue solid line. The blue dashed lines show the 68% confidence interval given by the 16th–84th inter-percentile range of the MCMC 'cloud' of possible fits. The described fitting procedure also allows estimating the probability that a given data point is an outlier to the obtained relation, i.e., an estimate of the posterior probability that each individual observation 'belongs' to the obtained relation. Such outliers can be due to for instance weather, bad calibration, image defects, etc. The data points represented by the open circles with the dashed error ellipses have a posterior probability of being outliers to the shown MCMC fit which is larger than 50%. On average 8% and 19% of the observed epochs were counted as outliers to the obtained relations when fitting in gr and ui-space respectively. Similar fits in gr (and ui) space were performed for all 9093 quasars in the Stripe 82 sample, each resulting in estimates for the gr and ui color variability for each object. Note that the temporal ordering of the flux points plays no role in this analysis.

Color Variability in gr

The immediate result of the MCMC fitting procedure; the directly observed gr color variability for the 9093 spectroscopically confirmed quasars from Stripe 82 as a function of their spectroscopic redshifts (left panel). It is clear that the vast majority of the quasars show color variability sgr < 0 (i.e., they get bluer when they brighten) represented by the shaded region. The right panel shows the analogous plot for the ui color variability, which we consider further. Figure shows that there is a very significant redshift dependence on the mean observed color variability, hsgr/uii(z). Spectra (Wilhite et al. 2005) and other information suggest that the hsgr/uii(z) behavior seen in Figure arises from a general trend of bluer continuum color in higher flux states modified by the redshift-dependent influence of emission lines in a given observed bandpass. As we will show in detail below, such a description is consistent with trends in the Stripe 82 data. The colors of quasars in general are known to have a pronounced redshift dependence resembling that seen in Figure because emission lines and the continuum affect static

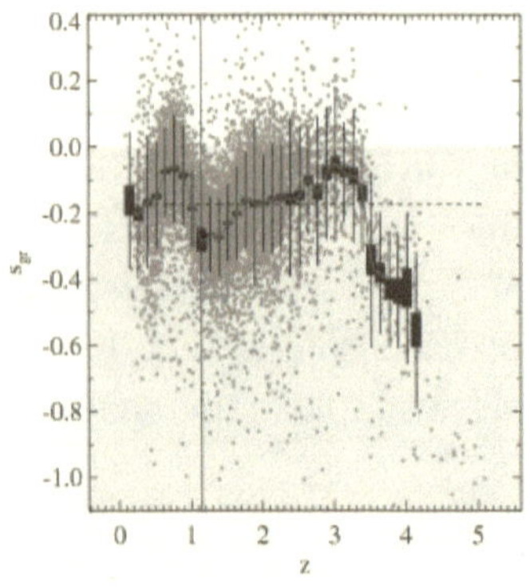

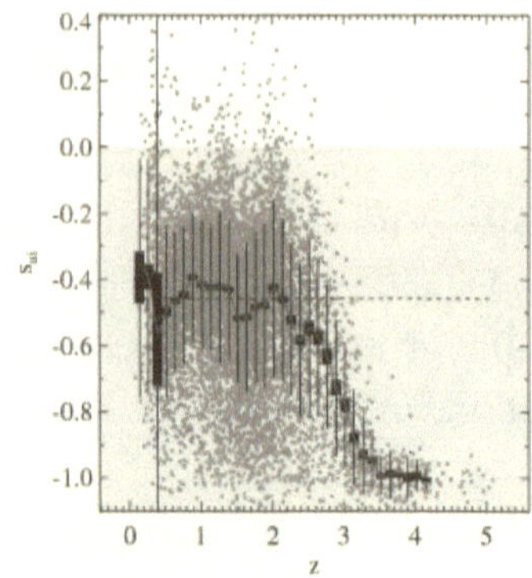

The color variability, sλ1λ2 , in gr (left) and ui-space (right) for the full sample of 9093 Stripe 82 quasars (dark gray dots), as a function of redshift. The black rectangles show the sample mean and its uncertainties in redshift bins of Δz = 0.125, containing at least 5 data points. The width (σ) of the color variability distribution is indicated by the thin error bars. The red curve gives the interpolated mean redshift trend, hsgri(z), and the black dashed line indicates the sample median color variability of -0.17 (-0.46) in gr (ui). The shaded region indicates where sgr and sui < 0, i.e., where bluer means brighter. The complex redshift-dependence of color variability is due to the influence of various emission lines.

or single epoch colors. For instance, the strong drop in hsgri(z) at z ~ 0.95 in Figure corresponds exactly to the redshift where the Mgii line moves from the g to the r band. This is illustrated, where the left panel shows the Vanden Berk et al. (2001) composite quasar spectrum from Figure with the 5 SDSS bands as they would be positioned if the quasar was at z = 0.95. The right panel shows the ratio between the emission line flux (Fline; the composite spectrum minus the estimated continuum flux) and the estimated continuum flux (Fcont; modeled as a simple power-law) as a function of redshift. The shift of the Mgii line from the g (green) to the r (yellow) band is marked. Likewise the dips and bumps in hsgri(z) at z ~ 1.85, 2.8 and 3.5 in the left panel of Figure are attributable to the Ciii], Civ and Lyα lines (see Figure) shifting between the g and r bands respectively. In the right panel of Figure is shown since this is the region where a simple single-power-law approximation of the continuum is valid. For higher redshift the g and r bands move blue-ward of the Lyα line.

In order to isolate the continuum color variability for comparison with other quantities such as Lbol/LEdd and MBH, we need to eliminate the source redshift dependence induced by the emission lines. This is done by 'emission line correcting' the individual values of sgr and sui by the quantity

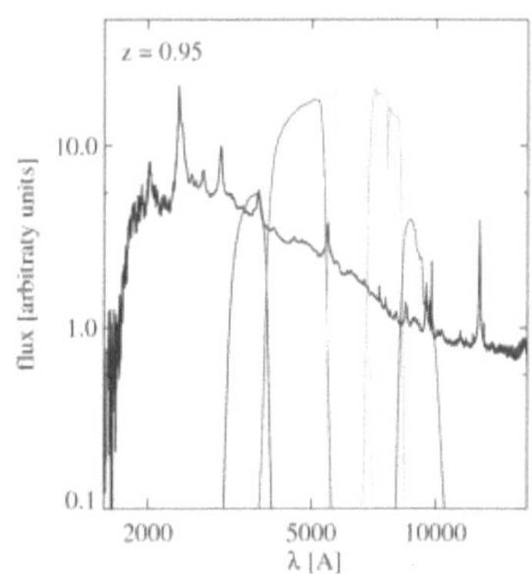

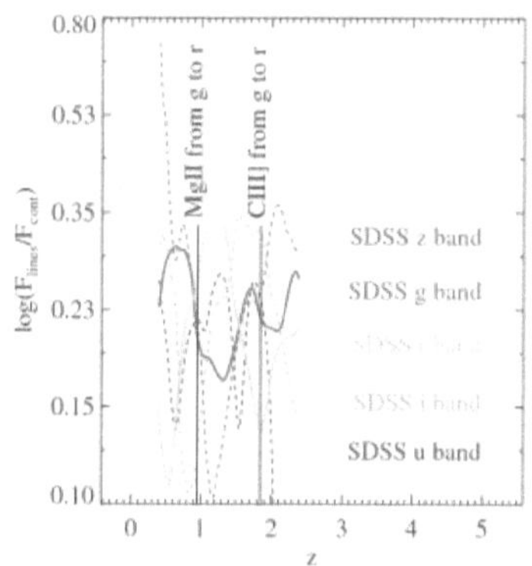

The role of emission lines in the color variability. On the left, the Vanden Berk et al. (2001) composite SDSS spectrum shown with the 5 SDSS filter's response curves (ugriz from left to right; arbitrarily scaled for visibility) as they would fall if the quasar was at z = 0.95. In the right panel the expected ratio between the line flux Fline and the continuum flux Fcont for the same spectrum is shown as a function of redshift with the SDSS g (green) and r (yellow) bands shown as solid curves and the u (blue), i (orange) and z (red) bands shown as dashed curves. The redshift at which the Mgii and Ciii] lines move from the g to the r band (z ~ 0.95 and z ~ 1.85 respectively) has been indicated. This illustrates the redshift dependence of the color variability seen in Figure and described in the text. The redshift range in the right panel has been set equal to the one used in Figure to ease comparison.

$$\langle s\rangle - \langle s_k\rangle(z) \quad .$$

Here the first term is the mean color variability of -0.17 (-0.46) in gr (ui) which is our stand-in for the emission line free color variability (dashed line(s) in Figure). The second term is the mean color variability for the sample capturing the mean redshift dependence of the sample as depicted by the red line in Figure for each of the individual quasars, k.

Reproducing the Color Variability Redshift Dependence with Simple Variability Model

We now quantify to which extent a simple spectral variability model can reproduce the observed redshift trends in hsgri(z). We do this by integrating a time-varying sequence of mock spectra created from the Vanden Berk et al. (2001) composite quasar spectrum over the SDSS g an r filters as illustrated in the left panel of Figure. After decomposing the Vanden Berk et al. (2001) spectrum in a continuum and line component, by subtracting the estimated power-law continuum from Vanden Berk et al. (2001) illustrated by the long-dashed line, we varied both the continuum and line flux to create a mock time sequence of spectra for which we obtained g and r light curves and then sgr. By changing the slope of the continuum (with a pivot-point in the infrared to ensure sgr < 0) and scaling the line response by a given amount, a sequence of spectra could be created to simulate a variable quasar. The line response was characterized by the ratio between the total integrated change in continuum flux and the total change in line flux over the modeled wavelength range

$$\alpha = \frac{\delta F_{\text{line}}}{\delta F_{\text{cont}}}$$

and could be set free (both lines and continuum can vary freely) or be fixed. Several setups for creating the sequence of variable spectra were inspected. Among those setups were fixed line contribution with changing continuum slope and both continuum and lines changing in various ways. For given α the emission lines are assumed to respond instantly to the continuum variation; i.e., in this simplistic approach we ignore any of the existing reverberation time-delay between the continuum and the lines mentioned.

The predictions of the spectral variability models are shown in Figure together with the estimated values of sgr, shaded regions, and the mean redshift dependence, hsgri(z), from the left panel of Figure. This Figure shows that hsgri(z) is best matched if the (implicitly instant) line response is very sub-linear: $\alpha = 0.1$ (purple line in Figure) is a much better fit than the model with $\alpha = 1$ (red line in Figure). It is seen that for emission lines that vary in lockstep with the continuum by $\alpha > 25\%$ the redshift features in hsgri(z) are 'inverted'. Actually, unresponsive line fluxes (i.e., $\alpha = 0$), lead to the best match in this model context (black dashed curve in Figure). Overall, Figure tells us that the redshift dependence of the gr color variability is nicely reproduced by a simple spectral variability model where the continuum of the spectrum is hardened, i.e., its power-law slope is changed so brighter makes bluer, and the emission line fluxes in the two bands are (instantly) unresponsive. As mentioned we know from detailed reverberation studies that emission lines do respond for quasars at z ~ 1. The explanation for α ≈ 0 may be that the lags in the lines are long enough to introduce a phase offset whereby the line is sometimes stronger, sometimes weaker than predicted from a tight correlation and in the net the correlation gets lost.

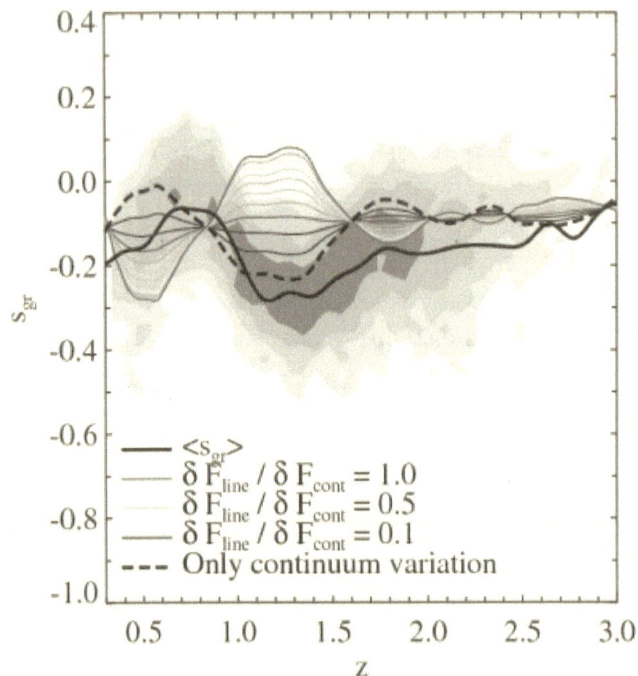

Comparison of the observed redshift dependence of sgr with our simple spectral variability models. The mean hsgri(z) is shown by the solid black line (cf. Figure). The rainbow colored curves show the color variability models with fixed ratios α (see Equation) between the line variability and continuum variability from a ratio of 0.1 (purple) to a ratio of α = 1.0 (red). The variability model, where only the continuum varies (α = 0) is shown as the dashed black line, providing the best match to the observations. Reverberation mapping timelags, ($\tau \sim 0.3 - 1$ year × $(1 + z)$ in quasars, e.g., Kaspi et al. 2007) are not taken into account.

model leads to the same conclusions and predicts the redshift behavior in Figure equally well for s‘ui.

Improved modeling, including a broken power-law continuum, explicit treatment of line reverberation and lack of variability at higher rest wavelengths as shown in Vanden Berk et al. (2004) and Wilhite et al. (2005), would be fruitful to carry out, but is beyond the scope of the present work.

Color Variability in ui

The SDSS Stripe 82 data offer the opportunity to extend this analysis beyond the relatively short spectral range covered by g and r, 4770 Å to 6231 Å in the observed frame. We do so by exploring the color variability in the u vs. i magnitude-magnitude space,

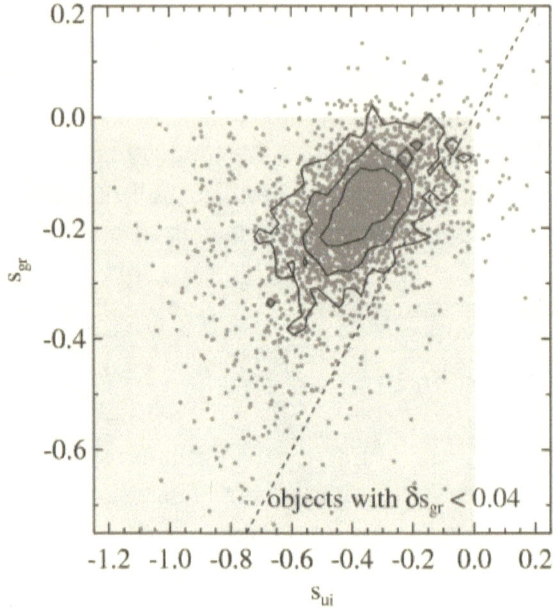

: The color variability in gr vs. ui color variability space, after correcting for the lineinduced redshift dependence. The gray shaded region shows where sλ1λ2 < 0, i.e., where bluer means brighter. The dashed line indicates sgr = sui for reference. The ui color variability is more pronounced on average than the gr color variability. Only the 3111 objects of the sample with δsgr < 0.04 are shown.

which covers a spectral range from 3543 Å to 7625 Å. We chose to use the i-band instead of z because of the significantly smaller photometric uncertainties in the i-band. The fitting procedure was exactly analogous to the case of gr color variability as described. The right panel of Figure shows the estimated ui color variability for the Stripe 82 quasar sample. Despite the larger scatter in sui at any given redshift we see similar features such as a distinct redshift dependence in hsuii(z) superimposed on quite dramatic overall color variability of -0.46. It is clear that the ui color variability is more pronounced than the gr color variability; hsuii(z) < hsgri(z). This holds true for the ensemble properties as well as for individual objects, as illustrated in Figure, where we plot the emission line corrected color variability in gr and ui. The fact that sui < sgr for almost all objects, implies that there is a relatively stronger blueing over the ui spectral range than over the smaller gr range. The same conclusion is reached when accounting for the difference in the wavelength baselines between gr and ui by normalizing sgr and sui with the corresponding wavelength ratio.

Color Variability as a Function of Eddington Luminosity and Black Hole Mass

All 9093 spectroscopically confirmed quasars have matches in the quasar catalog presented in Shen et al. (2011), of which 99.9% (9088) have an estimate of the bolometric luminosity and 84.1% (7615) have an estimated black hole mass derived from Mgii. This allows us to normalize the bolometric luminosity to the Eddington luminosity (LEdd; Equation) to obtain the Eddington ratio.

If we plot the emission line corrected gr color variability against Lbol/LEdd and MBH, as shown in Figure, it is evident that there is no detectable relation between the color variability sgr and the Lbol/LEdd or MBH. This is also illustrated in Figure where a 2D histogram of Lbol/LEdd and MBH, with the bins color coded according to the median sgr, is shown: across the well sampled range in Lbol/LEdd and MBH, the median sgr varies by no more than 0.01 as a function of these two variables about the mean value of -0.17. The 2D histogram has been smoothed by a 2D gaussian to reflect the uncertainty in luminosity and mass, with the full width at half maximum of the smoothing kernel (represented by the ellipse in the bottom left of Figure) FWHM = [FWHM(MBH), FWHM(Lbol/LEdd)] = [0.35, 0.24] corresponding to [σ(MBH), σ(Lbol/LEdd)] = [0.15 dex, 0.1 dex]. Plots similar to the ones shown in Figure for the ui color variability show no significant Lbol/LEdd or MBH dependence, either. In Figure the full sample, i.e., all masses and redshifts are shown. Inspecting smaller subsamples in z (and MBH) space does not change the picture. Hence, we find no correlation between the color variability in gr (and ui) with Lbol/LEdd or MBH. More broadly, this seems to imply that the overall state of the quasar (characterized by Lbol/LEdd and MBH) plays no significant role in determining the color variability

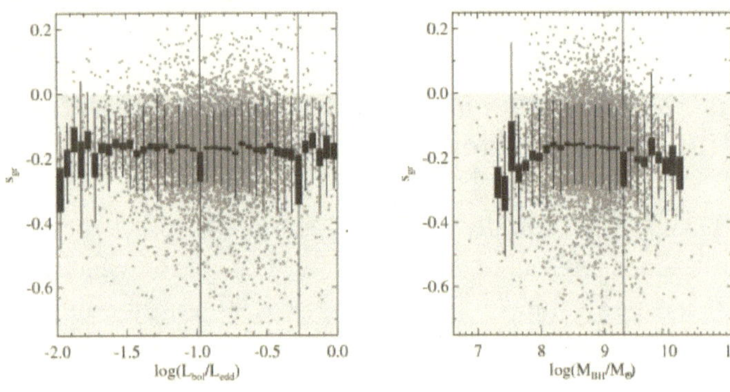

The emission line corrected gr color variability as a function of L'bol/L'Edd (left) and M'BH/M (right). The black rectangles indicate the mean sgr and its error in each L and MBH bin. The thin error bars show the width of the sgr distribution similar to in Figure. No correlation between the color variability and L'bol/L'Edd and M'BH/M is detected. This implies that the color variability is not a function of black hole mass or the overall (Eddington) accretion rate

The Color Variability as a Function of the Light Curve Variability Characteristics

We characterized the r-band variability of all the 9093 quasars through a structure function with an amplitude parameter A and the light curve stochasticity, γ. The structure function variability of each individual quasar was modeled by a simple power-law

$$SF_{mod}(\Delta t_{obs}|A, \gamma) = A\left(\frac{\Delta t_{obs}}{1\mathrm{yr}}\right)^{\gamma},$$

with Δtobs being the time between the observation of two individual photometric epochs and SFmod = p h(m(t1) – m(t2))2 i. The structure function of a periodically varying object or one varying like white noise will as mentioned have a flat structure function and hence a small power-law exponent γ (see Figure). Thus a large γ indicates a secularly varying object or an object with a random walk like variability. The latter has been shown to describe quasar variability well in Kelly et al. (2009) and MacLeod et al. (2011). The amplitude A corresponds to the average variability on a 1 year timescale. However, the spectroscopic redshift of each of the 9093 Stripe 82 quasars is known, and the amplitude can be corrected for time-dilation. The rest-frame variability amplitude A 0 is defined to be A(1 + z) γ such

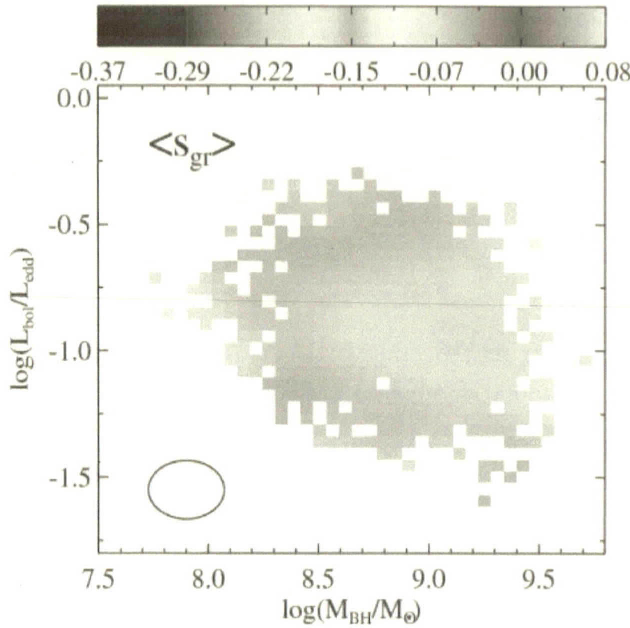

The color variability sgr as a function of L'bol/L'Edd and M'BH/M, as in Figure, again showing no significant trends. The color coding indicates the emission line corrected median gr color variability of the objects in the bin. To reflect the uncertainty in luminosity and mass, the distribution has been smoothed by a 2D gaussian (represented by the ellipse in the bottom left corner) with full width at half maximum of FWHM = [FWHM(MBH), FWHM(Lbol/LEdd)] = [0.35, 0.24] corresponding to [σ(M'BH), σ(L'bol/L'Edd)] = [0.15 dex, 0.1 dex].

$$SF_{mod}(\Delta t_{rest}|A', \gamma) = A' \left(\frac{\Delta t_{rest}}{1 yr} \right)^{\gamma} ,$$

where Δtrest is now the difference between observations in the quasar rest-frame. All quoted A 0 s are estimated from the robust r-band measurements as described. The variability amplitudes are independent of redshift in agreement with Giveon et al. (1999) and the majority of the previous studies listed in their Table.

In the following, however, the structure function parameters A and γ have been obtained. Rather than fitting the structure function directly to the magnitude differences we fit a Gaussian Process model (Rasmussen & Williams 2006) defined by the structure function to the magnitudes directly. This properly includes all of the correlations between data points. This Gaussian Process model consists of an n-dimensional Gaussian distribution (for n epochs) with a constant mean m and n × n variance matrix V. The elements of this variance matrix are given by

$$V_{ij} \equiv V(|t_i - t_j|) = V(\Delta t_{ij}) = \frac{1}{2}\left[\mathrm{SF}^2_{ij}(\infty) - \mathrm{SF}^2_{ij}(\Delta t_{ij})\right]$$

for data points at epochs ti and tj . Here the structure function SFi j is given by

$$\mathrm{SF}_{ij} = \sqrt{\langle (m(t_i) - m(t_j))^2 \rangle} \quad .$$

The photometric uncertainty variances are added to the diagonal elements of V. For the power-law structure function we cut off the power-law at 10 years such that SF(∞) is finite. As all data span less than 10 years this cut-off does not influence the fit. This type of fit is similar to the Ornstein-Uhlenbeck process describing quasar variability as a damped random walk.

We can now look at the emission line corrected sgr and sui as a function of A 0 and γ for all quasars. Figure 3.10 shows that sgr and sui seemingly vary both with A 0 and with γ. However, the limit of little variability (small A 0) requires particular care, both because outliers play a bigger role and because A 0 and γ starts to be degenerate. We estimated the gr color variability of 500 color-selected non-varying F/G stars and of the 483 Stripe 82 RR Lyrae stars from Sesar et al. (2010). These are over-plotted in the top panel of Figure as the blue and red points, respectively. As expected the RR Lyrae have a well defined color variability, whereas the inferred color variability of the non-varying F/G stars span a much wider range of sgr. Interestingly, the majority of the non-varying F/G stars have color variability estimates of sgr < 0 like the quasars and the RR Lyrae stars. This seems to be caused by the outliers in g being relatively larger than the outliers in r, hence affecting the initial guess of the MCMC in a bluer-brighter direction. In the case of the RR Lyrae the well defined mean color variability in gr is expected, as RR Lyrae change their effective temperature and luminosity during their pulsation. By creating a sequence of black body spectra with temperatures from 6200K to 7200K, estimating the flux received in the g and r bands for each spectrum, and using that as a simple model for a variable RR Lyrae star, a color variability of sgr ~ -0.23 is obtained, in very good agreement with the observations (top panel, red dots). Thus, in general the sgr for the F/G and RR Lyrae stars look as expected.

A more direct way to estimate the fidelity of color variability estimates at low A 0 values is to recover sgr estimates for objects of known (simulated) color variability. We induce such simulated variability into the 500 F/G stars by generating data of a certain 1 year amplitude (A 0) from the original F/G star g and r photometry. We do that by generating new u, g,r and i magnitudes for the individual epochs j via the expression

$$p_{j,\text{sim}} = p_j + A'_{\text{sim}} \frac{\Delta \text{MJD}_j}{365.25} \quad ,$$

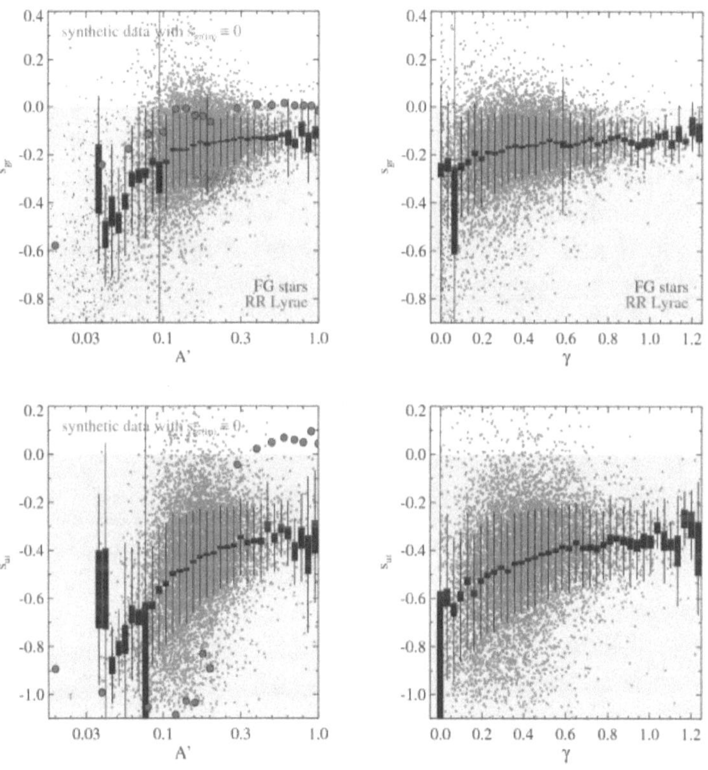

Correlation between the light curve (temporal variability) structure function and color variability. The emission line corrected color variability in gr (top) and ui (bottom) are plotted against A0 (left) and γ (right). A0 indicates the mean level of variability within one year (rest-frame), and γ, the power law exponent in the structure function, indicates how random (low γ) or secular (high γ) the light curve variations are. Gray dots (data), black rectangles and error bars are analogous to Figure. In the gr plots (top) 500 non-varying F/G stars and the 483 RR Lyrae from Sesar et al. (2010) are shown on top of the 9093 Stripe 82 quasars (gray dots) as blue and red points respectively. In the left column the recovered average sgr (sui) for 50 F/G stars is shown as green filled circles, where synthetic brightness variations with sgr(in) ≡ 0 and different variability amplitudes A0 sim have been created. As described in the text, this illustrates that only gr (ui) trends for A0 & 0.1 (A0 & 0.25) can and should be trusted. It shows that objects with large A0 , i.e., with large variability amplitudes, have a color variability close(r) to 0, i.e., less blueing when brightening, than do objects with small A0 . The trends in the two right hand plots are dominated by low A0 objects and is therefore not trustworthy.

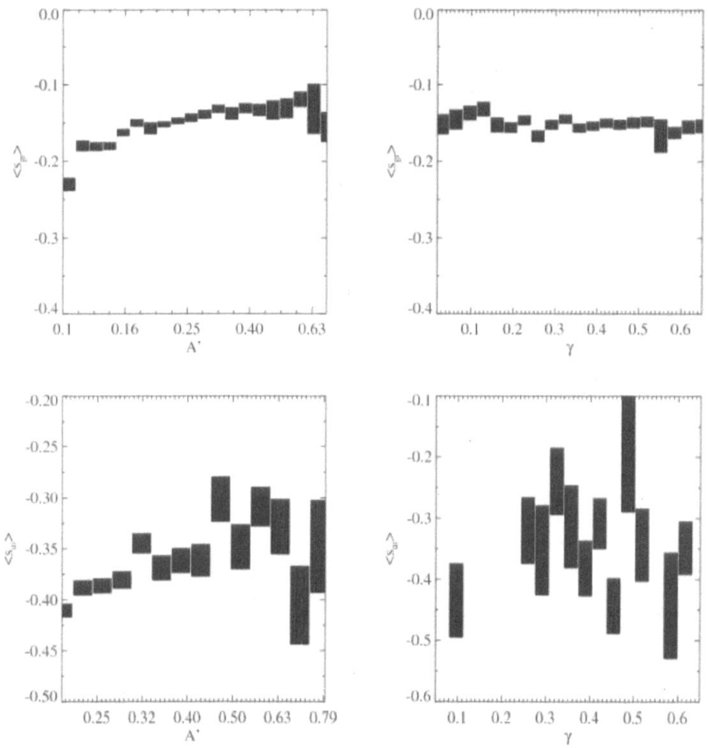

The estimated correlations between mean color variability and structure function parameters. The four panels show the portion of parameter space in Figure that is well populated by the sample. The rectangles in the left hand plots correspond to the ones in Figure. In the right hand plots the rectangles are only estimated from objects with A0 > 0.1 (0.25). A clear trend is seen, that the color variability of objects with high variability amplitude are closer to 0 than objects with small variability amplitude (left panel). This indicates that strongly varying quasars get less blue as they brighten on average, than do moderate varying quasars. The color variability is independent of the power law index γ.The estimated correlations between mean color variability and structure function parameters. The four panels show the portion of parameter space in Figure that is well populated by the sample. The rectangles in the left hand plots correspond to the ones in Figure. In the right hand plots the rectangles are only estimated from objects with A0 > 0.1 (0.25). A clear trend is seen, that the color variability of objects with high variability amplitude are closer to 0 than objects with small variability amplitude (left panel). This indicates that strongly varying quasars get less blue as they brighten on average, than do moderate varying quasars. The color variability is independent of the power law index γ.

which by construction is a data set with s = 0. Here p represents the photometric measurements in a given band, j runs over the individual epochs, and ΔMJDj refers to the observation time of the jth epoch with respect to the first observation. In this way many of the aspects of the real data (i.e., the outliers and realistic photometric errors) are included in the simulated data. In the two left panels of Figure this recovered mean average (over 50 randomly chosen F/G stars) color variability is shown for a sequence

of variability amplitudes, A 0 sim, as large filled green circles. This shows that the recovered gr (ui) color variability has some systematic errors below A 0 . 0.1 (A 0 . 0.25). When ignoring quasars with variability amplitudes smaller than 0.1 (0.25) the correlation between sgr and sui and A 0 is still present and significant. The trustworthy part of the relations, hsgri(A, γ) and hsuii(A, γ), in Figure is shown in Figure. Again the black rectangles represent the uncertainty on the estimated mean color variability. The left hand plots correspond directly to Figure, whereas for hsgri(γ) and hsuii(γ) the black rectangles are estimated only from objects with A 0 > 0.1 (A 0 > 0.25). Figure clearly illustrates the trend that objects with larger variability amplitude have a smaller color variability (meaning less blueing when brightening) than for low A 0 . On the other hand the color variability is independent of γ.

Color Variability of Individual Quasars vs. the Color Distribution of Quasar Ensembles

The colors of quasars at a given redshift are known to depend only weakly on their mean accretion luminosity or accretion rate, while we find that individual quasars become considerably bluer when they brighten on year time-scales. This suggests different physical mechanisms creating the accretion luminosity range in ensembles and the luminosity variations in individual quasars.

In figure the emission line corrected color variability of a sub-sample of the Stripe 82 quasars is shown in gr and ui-space. This sub-sample represents the 'average' quasars, i.e., the combined sample of the 33rd–66th percentile of masses and the 25th–75th percentile of redshifts for the quasar sample. The color variability of each individual quasar is depicted as a short solid gray line showing s 0 gr (s 0 ui) from Equation for each quasar centered on [hgi,hri] ([hui,hii]) for that particular quasar. Only every 10th object of the sub-sample is actually shown to keep the individual gray lines visible. The length of the lines resemble the change in the photometric g-band (u-band) data of the quasar. The Figure compares the average s 0 gr (s 0 ui) of all the individual quasars in the sub-sample (red solid line) with a fit to the time-averaged color distribution of the subsample (black solid line) where each data point corresponds to [hgi,hri]k ([hui,hii]k) with k counting the quasars. Figure reveals that indeed the mean color variability for individual quasars is much more pronounced than the equivalent quantity for the ensemble, ssample = dhmri dhmgi . For the given sub-sample sgr ~ −0.18 and sui ~ −0.48 on average (as opposed to sgr ~ −0.17 and sui ~ −0.46) compared to sgr = −0.01 and sui ~ −0.08 for the corresponding time-averaged sub-sample color distribution. The difference is highly significant in both cases, with the ui color variability difference formally larger, because of the broader spectral range. The exact same trends are found for plots containing the full quasar sample.

This result shows that (temporal) color variability of individual quasars is considerably stronger than the color range of ensembles of quasars at similar redshifts and with similar black hole masses, that presumably differ in L'bol/L'Edd.

Color Variability vs. Accretion Disk Models

Explaining quasar spectral energy distributions, and in particular the UV/optical continuum through steady-state accretion disk models has an established history. However, comparing the observed color variability of large samples of quasars with the predicted colors of model sequences of varying accretion rate has not been done yet. Such a comparison could tell us whether it is sensible to think of the quasar variability on scales of years as changes in the mean accretion rate. The superb Stripe 82 data enables us to perform such a comparison, by comparing the observed color and color variability of the Stripe 82 quasars with sequences of accretion disk models presented in Davis et al. (2007).

Davis et al. (2007) presented three different thin accretion disk models that describe the spectral slope of quasars as a function of L'bol/L'Edd and M'BH. We took these three models and worked out predictions for the observed g and r band for models of a given M'BH but varying accretion rates. The three models presented in Davis et al. (2007) and the color we adopt for their graphical representation are:

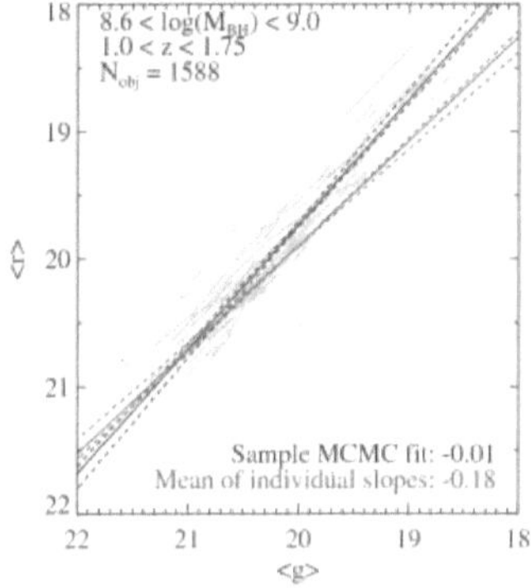

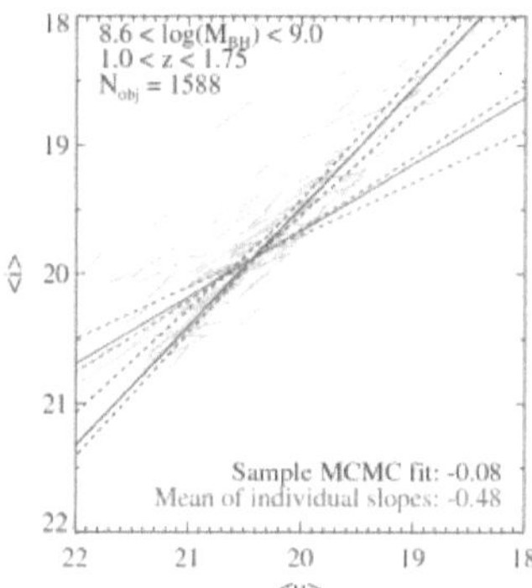

The color variability in individual quasars (red) vs. the color-luminosity relation in the ensemble of quasars (black), drawing on the sub-sample of 33rd–66th percentile of masses and the 25th–75th percentile of redshifts. The mass and redshift ranges are shown in each panel. Each individual quasar is indicated by a short solid gray line corresponding to the fitted and emission line corrected gr (ui) relation, with a length reflecting the standard deviation of the g (u) light curve. Only every 10th object of the sub-sample is shown to keep the individual objects visible. The red solid lines show the average trend within this sub-sample of sgr ~ −0.18 and sui ~ −0.48, with the dashed red lines indicating the bootstrapping uncertainty. The black lines show a MCMC fit to the time-averaged fluxes for the sample, i.e., the fit to (hgi,hri) ± (stdev(g),stdev(r)) for each quasar, corresponding to sgr ~ −0.01 and sui ~ −0.08. The dashed black lines show the 68% confidence interval of the MCMC fit. In other words, the red line is the ensemble mean color variability while the black line is a fit to the ensemble of time-averaged mean magnitudes. Hence, it is clear that the average color variability of the individual quasars deviate significantly from the time averaged sample color variability.

1) A relativistic model of accretion onto a Schwarzschild black hole with a spin parameter of 0. The emission is based on Non-LTE atmosphere calculations (green).

2) A relativistic model of accretion onto a Schwarzschild black hole with a spin parameter of 0. The disk is emitting as a black body (red).

3) A Model of accretion onto a spinning black hole (spin parameter of 0.9) with emission based on Non-LTE atmosphere calculations (orange).

For further details on the models we refer to Davis et al. (2007). We can compare the models to the data in two respects:

(i) do they predict the right color (which has been done before) and

(ii) do they predict the right change of color with changing accretion rate or luminosity? In Figure the quasar from Figure is shown in g-r-(g−r) space (without error ellipses) together with its best fit color variability

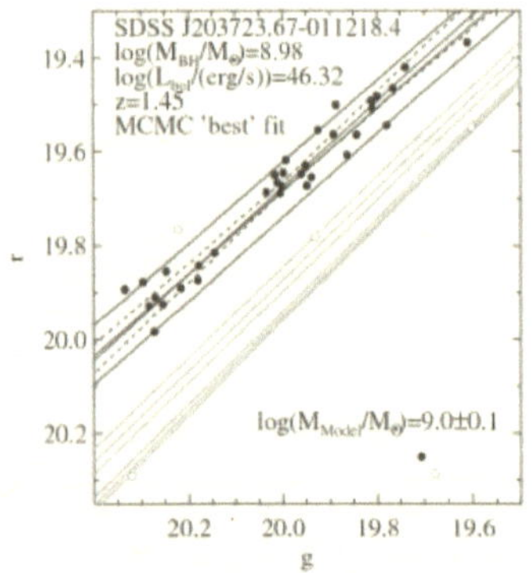

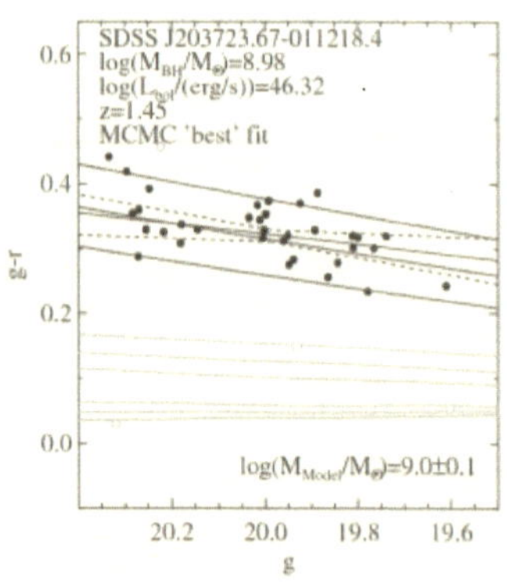

Comparison of the observed color variability with sequences of steady-state accretion disk models of different accretion rates. This comparison is illustrated using the quasar SDSS J2037-0112 from Figure, shown in r vs. g (left) and g − r vs. g (right) space. The black symbols are the individual photometric measurements. The blue solid line shows the MCMC fit in gr-space to these measurements and the blue dashed lines indicate the 68% confidence interval of that fit. The open symbols denote likely outliers. The Davis et al. (2007) models described are shown in green (model 1), red (model 2) and orange (model 3) with L'bol/ L'Edd changing along the lines. Each set of 3 lines denotes models for differing black hole masses near the value determined from the Mgii line width (Shen et al. 2011). From top to bottom each set of lines (models) correspond to 9.1, 9.0 and 8.9 log(Mmodel/M).

(blue solid line). The three accretion disk models are shown as solid lines in bundles of three, where each of the three lines corresponds to a different black hole mass, as noted in the bottom right corner of each panel. In this particular case model 2) matches the data well both in color and in the change of color with changing luminosity. However, such a good match is not representative for the ensemble. We quantify this for the whole sample by estimating the 'goodness' of the models as:

$$\mathbf{D}_y = \left(\sum_j^{N_k} \frac{1}{\delta y_j}\right)^{-1} \sum_j^{N_k} \frac{y_j - y(x)_{j,\mathrm{model}}}{\delta y_j}$$

$$\Delta s = s_k - s_{k,\mathrm{model}} \,,$$

where y = (g − r) and x = g. The index j runs over the Nk epochs for each individual quasar k. The model prediction is the color at a given luminosity (or accretion rate), for a fixed black hole mass y(x)j,model. The photometric error on the color for the jth measurement is denoted by δyj . Since the error on the M'BH estimates based on Mgii is ~ 0.4 dex, we have chosen to show three values for MBH, leading to three model prediction lines, for each model in Figure. The 'goodness' parameters Dy and Δs defined in above Equations therefore describe how well the observed values of color and color variability are predicted by the Davis et al. (2007) models. Dy can be seen as the standard χ 2 measure of comparison between model and data before squaring, i.e., it estimates the difference between the model color and the observed color averaged over all epochs for each quasar. The Δs is simply the difference between model color variability and observed color variability of each quasar.

Figure summarizes the model–data comparison for a subset of quasars with z ~ 1.5: the quantities from Equations. All models predict a color variability – as a function of changes in the mean accretion rate – that is weaker than observed. On average model 2) shown in red matches the observed gr color variability the best. Furthermore, the Dg–r values indicate that the g – r color is on average overestimated by model 1) and 3), whereas the distribution of model 2) has a mean very close to the dashed perfect agreement line. Creating similar plots for other mass and redshift ranges as well as for the results in ui-space show the exact same trends. Thus, of the three Davis et al. (2007) accretion disk models considered here, model 2) matches the observed color and the obtained gr and ui color variability the best.

CHAPTER FOUR

Star Formation in High Redshift Galaxy Mergers

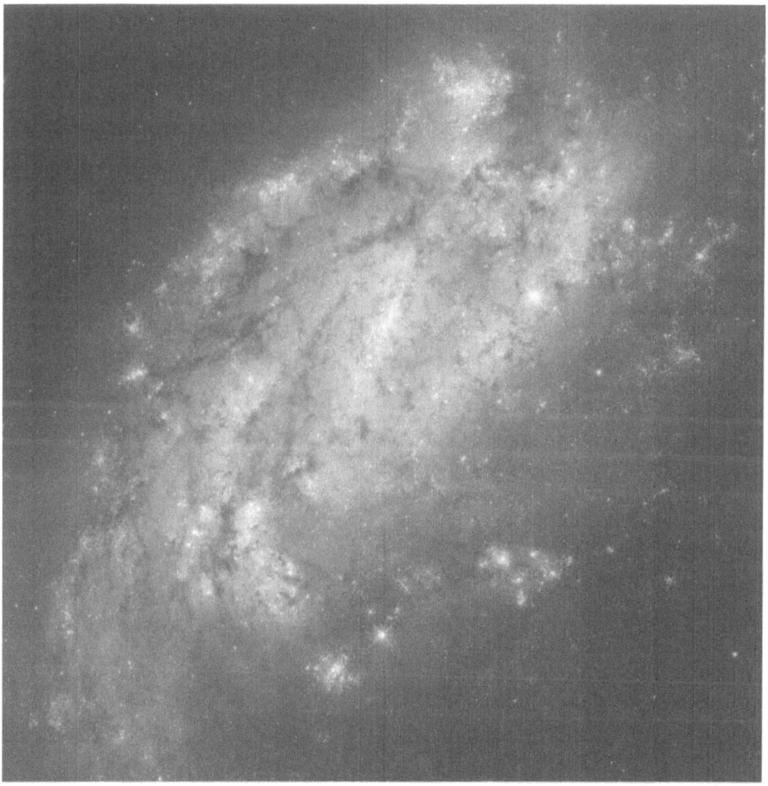

In this chapter we will present and analyze the spatial distribution of star formation in an extensive sample of galaxy mergers at z > 1. Our sample, drawn from the 3D-HST survey, is the first merger sample to be systematically selected at these redshifts and consists of 61 objects, including pre-mergers (close pairs) and post-mergers (single objects with multiple components and/or tidal features). Total stellar masses and star formation rates are derived from multi-wavelength photometry. The slitless spectra from 3D-HST provide emission line maps, which are projected back onto the undispersed continuum images, providing a comprehensive, high-resolution, empirical picture of where star formation happens in galaxy mergers at the epoch where the cosmic star formation rate density peaked. We find that detectable star formation can occur in one (or both) galaxy centers, or in tidal tails. The most common case (69%) is that star formation is largely concentrated in a single, compact region, coincident with a peak in rest-frame optical continuum emission. This suggests that z ~ 1.5 mergers typically occur between galaxies with different gas fractions. No correlations between star formation morphology and redshift, total stellar mass, or star formation rate is found. An initial comparison with a restricted set of cosmological hydrodynamical simulations of mergers between similarly massive and gas-rich objects, supports this by predicting that star formation usually occurs in both components of the merger, when the gas fraction of the individual components is the same.

Numerical technique

The coarsest grid is composed of 643 cells in a cubic box of 200 kpc, and we allow up to 10 further levels of refinement. This results in a maximum spatial resolution of 6 pc. Star and dark matter (DM) particles are also implemented in the initial conditions. We call the former old stars, to differentiate them from the new stars, that are formed during the simulation. A grid cell is refined if when there are more than 40 initial condition particles, or if the baryonic mass, including gas, old and new stars, exceeds 8 × 10‘5 M⊙. Furthermore, we ensure that the Jeans length is always resolved by at least four cells, by introducing a numerical pressure through a temperature floor set by a polytrope equation of state at high density (T∝ρ2), which is called Jeans polytrope thereafter, which prevents numerical fragmentation.

The thermodynamical model, including heating and atomic cooling at solar metallicity,1 is the same as described in Renaud et al. (2015).

If the gas reaches a certain density threshold, ρ0, and if its temperature is no more than 2 × 104 K above the Jeans polytrope temperature at the corresponding density, it is converted into stellar particles following a Schmidt law, ρ˙⋆=ϵ(ρgas/tff), with ε the efficiency per free fall time set to 1 per cent, and

$$t_{\text{ff}} = \sqrt{3\pi/(32G\rho)}$$

the free-fall time. The density thresholds (ρ0 = 30 cm−3 and ρ0 = 1e5 cm−3 for low and high gas fraction cases) are chosen to correspond to the isolated discs being on the disc sequence of the Schmidt–Kennicutt diagram, that is an SFR of ≃ 1M⊙ yr−1 (resp. ≃60M⊙ yr−1) in the low gas fraction case for each galaxy before the interaction. The difference in the normalization of ρ0 originates from the different gas mean density between the two cases.2

Because of the spatial resolution and the computational cost it would imply, we do not resolve individual star formation. We chose a high enough sampling mass for the new stars, i.e. higher than 1000 M⊙, so that we do not need to resolve the initial mass function.

In these simulations, we model three types of stellar feedback.

* Photoionization from H II regions (as in Renaud et al. 2013): UV photons from the OB-type stars ionize the surrounding gas. To model this process, we evaluate the radius of the Strömgren (1939)

sphere around the newly formed stellar particle and heat up the gas to T'H II=2×104 K.

* Radiation pressure (as in Renaud et al. 2013): inside each H II region, the scattering of photons on the gas acts as a radiative pressure. To model this process, we inject a radial velocity kick for each cell inside the Stromgren sphere.

* Type-II supernova (SN) thermal blasts stars more massive than 4 M⊙ eventually explode as Type II SNe (Povich 2012). We assume that 20 per cent of the initial mass of our stellar particle is in massive stars, and will be released 10 Myr after the formation of the stellar particle. On top of the mass-loss, we inject thermally a certain amount of energy in the cell: ESN = 1051 erg/10 M⊙.

This implementation of stellar feedback is therefore physically motivated, although subgrid. It has been used in numerical simulations of high gas fraction disc galaxies similar to ours, and was shown to have realistic effects on the galaxies, such as producing large-scale outflows with a mass-loading factor close to unity (Roos et al. 2015)

Modelling low- and high-redshift galactic discs

We run a suite of massive galaxy merger simulations for gas-rich (fgas = 60 per cent) and gas-poor discs (fgas = 10 per cent). These gas fractions are typical of z = 2 and 0 disc galaxies. We chose to modify solely the gas fraction in order to isolate the effect of this parameter, and neglect the other differences between the low- and high-redshift, such as galaxy size, mass, and interaction parameters. These parameters are discussed Furthermore, it must be noted that we do not change the stellar mass of the bulge, so that the velocity profile and the galactic shear stay the same, and so that the low and high gas fraction orbits are as similar as possible.

The DM halo for each galaxy is composed of 2.62 × 105 M⊙ particles. An old stellar component is added, made of 9 × 104 M⊙ particles modelling a stellar disc and a stellar bulge. The characteristics of the galaxies are summed up in Table. The DM, old stars, and the stellar particles formed during the simulation are evolved through a particle-mesh solver, with a gravitational softening of 50 pc for the DM and old stars and at the resolution of the local resolution for the new stars.

Table 1. Characteristics of the galaxies used in the simulations.

Galaxy	**Low gas fraction**	**High gas fraction**
Total baryonic mass ($\times 10^9$ $M_\odot$)	57.2	
Gas disc (exponential profile)		
Mass ($\times 10^9$ $M_\odot$)	5.0	34.3
Characteristic radius (kpc)	8.0	
Truncation radius (kpc)	14.0	
Characteristic height (kpc)	0.3	
Truncation height (kpc)	0.8	
Stellar disc (exponential profile)		
Number of particles	500 000	173 900
Mass ($\times 10^9$ $M_\odot$)	45.0	15.7
Characteristic radius (kpc)	5.0	
Truncation radius (kpc)	12.0	
Characteristic height (kpc)	0.34	

Characteristic radius (kpc)	5.0
Truncation radius (kpc)	12.0
Characteristic height (kpc)	0.34
Truncation height (kpc)	1.02
Bulge (Hernquist profile)	
Number of particles	80 000
Mass ($\times 10^9$ $M_\odot$)	7.2
Characteristic radius (kpc)	1.3
Truncation radius (kpc)	3.0
DM halo (Burkert profile)	
Number of particles	500 000
Mass ($\times 10^9$ $M_\odot$)	131.0
Characteristic radius (kpc)	25.0
Truncation radius (kpc)	45.0

Characteristics of the orbits

Our simulation sample comprises three orbits. Their parameters are summarized in Tables 2 and 3. The full simulation suite is summarized in Table 4. Low and high gas fraction mergers are run on the same reference orbit #1 for comparison. This orbit is close to that of the Antennae system, which was shown by R14 to be favourable to a strong starburst for low gas fraction discs. Orbits #2 and #3 have lower orbital energy, obtained by reducing the impact parameter and relative velocity by 15 and 30 per cent. This ensures that the results do not depend on an unforeseen particularity of the orbit. The initial orbital conditions are summarized in Table 2.

Table 2. Initial conditions of the orbits.

	Galaxy 1	**Galaxy 2**
Orbit #1		
Centre (kpc)	(10.55, −30.34, 46.68)	(−15.01, 30.44, −46.34)
Velocity (km s^{-1})	(−26.95, 23.23, −71.76)	(26.02, −23.28, 71.35)
Orbit #2		
Centre (kpc)	(8.64, −25.78, 39.71)	(−13.10, 25.89, −39.36)
Velocity (km s^{-1})	(−22.98, 19.74, −61.03)	(22.05, −19.80, 60.61)
Orbit #3		
Centre (kpc)	(6.21, −20.01, 30.87)	(−10.67, 20.11, −30.52)
Velocity (km s^{-1})	(−17.94, 15.32, −47.43)	(17.01, −15.37, 47.02)

Table 3. Orientations of the spin axis.

Spin	**Galaxy 1**	**Galaxy 2**
dd	(−0.67, −0.71, 0.20)	(0.65, 0.65, −0.40)
rr	(0.67, 0.71, −0.20)	(−0.65, −0.65, 0.40)
Spin1	(−0.67, 0.71, −0.20)	(−0.65, 0.65, 0.40)
Spin2	(0.67, −0.71, 0.20)	(−0.65, −0.65, 0.40)
Spin3	(0.67, 0.71, 0.20)	(0.65, −0.65, 0.40)
Spin4	(−0.67, 0.71, −0.20)	(−0.65, −0.65, −0.40)

Table 4. Summary of the simulations. The prefix 'gp' stands for gas-poor. dd and rr stand for direct-direct and retrograde-retrograde, and are followed by the number of the corresponding orbit.

Name	Orbit	Spins	Gas fraction	Maximum resolution (pc)
Iso	-	-	60%	6
gp-iso	-	-	10%	6
dd1	1	dd	60%	6
rr1	1	rr	60%	6
gp-dd1	1	dd	10%	6
gp-rr1	1	rr	10%	6
dd2	2	dd	60%	12
rr2	2	rr	60%	12
Spin1	2	Spin1	60%	12
Spin2	2	Spin2	60%	12
Spin3	2	Spin3	60%	12
Spin4	2	Spin4	60%	12
dd3	3	dd	60%	12
rr3	3	rr	60%	12

As the orientation of the galaxies plays a significant role in the processes at play (see the review by Duc & Renaud 2013), we use a set of different spin vectors for each orbit (see Table 3). For each orbit, we run one direct–direct, Antennae-like interaction and one retrograde–retrograde encounter. The latter is obtained by merely taking the opposite of the spin orientation of both galaxies. To ensure that the different spin-orbit couplings do not affect our conclusions, we also run four other simulations with a different spin orientation on orbit #2.

We run orbit #1 simulations at 6 pc resolution and orbits #2 and #3 at 12 pc resolution, using the same refinement strategy as for the 6 pc case, stopped one level lower, and ρ0 = 1e4 cm−3 as star formation threshold, which is lower than for the 6 pc resolution as the mean density is also lower.

Galaxy morphologies

Fig. shows a gas density map of the isolated run of both modelled disc galaxies. We see that while the low gas fraction disc shows several gaseous spiral arms, the high gas fraction disc is fragmented in several dense regions. These gaseous regions are observed to be long-lived.[3] They undergo merging and migration towards the centre with characteristic time of several 100 Myr. We will call them clumps thereafter.

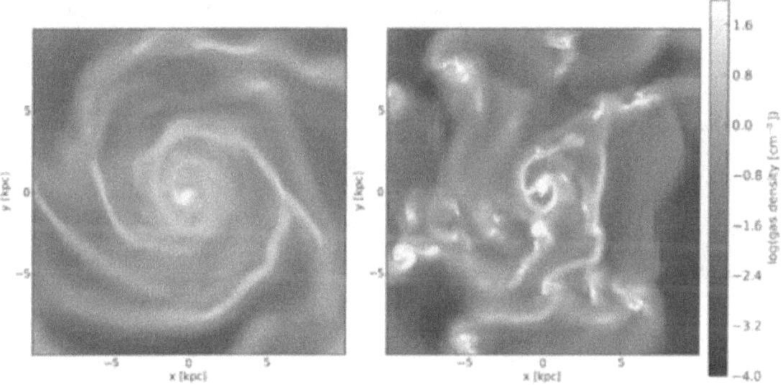

Face-on mass-weighted mean gas density maps of the isolated runs: gp-iso is shown on the left-hand panel and iso on the right-hand panel. Both maps are obtained after an evolution during the time corresponding to the first pericentre for orbit #1 (490 Myr after the start of the simulation).

Here in next fig we show the gas density map of the merger in the low and high gas fraction case for orbit #1 (dd1 and gp-dd1) at different times of the interaction; a few 10 Myr before and after both the first pericentre passage and the coalescence. We see that the gas in the low gas fraction case shows the formation of a few clumps in the tidal bridge after the first pericentre passage. On the bottom row, the evolution of the gas density of the high gas fraction case does not show any significant increase in the number of clumps before and after the first pericentre passage.

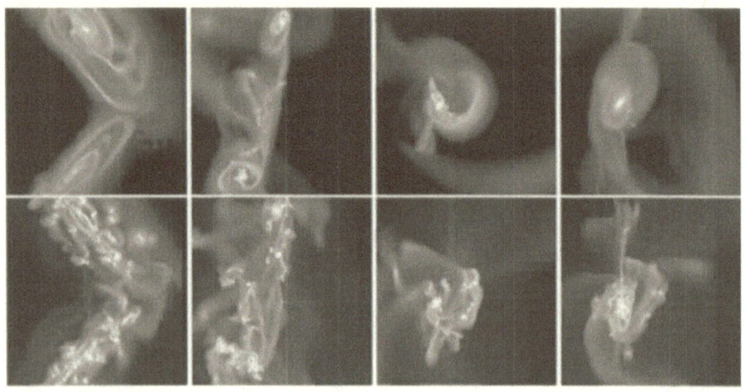

Mass-weighted mean gas density map of the gas-poor (top panel) and gas-rich (bottom panel) simulations for the direct–direct interaction orbit #1 at different times from the first pericentre : −60, 105, 370, and 560 Myr from left to right. The maps span an area of 30 kpc × 30 kpc. The colour scale is the same as before Fig.

To have a more quantitative insight into the interaction-driven clumpiness of the disc, we use the friend-of-friend algorithm HOP (Eisenstein & Hut 1998) to determine the number of clumps and the gas mass fraction embedded in them, during the interaction. Clumps are detected around peaks of gas density above 40 cm−3. Subclumps are merged if the saddle density between them exceeds 4 cm−3 and an outer boundary of 2 cm−3 is set to define the density limit of the clumps. These parameters agree with a visual examination of the density maps and the results are not affected with respect to small changes of these parameters.

In Next Fig., we show the evolution of the number of clumps, and the gas fraction inside them. In the low gas fraction case, the gas fraction enclosed in clumps goes from 5 to 25 per cent at the first pericentre passage, and the number of clumps increases by a factor of 4, from about 4 to 16. These numbers stay relatively constant along the interaction. This enhanced number of clumps in low-redshift galaxy collisions has been already noted. In the high gas fraction case, the gas mass fraction in clumps shows instead a slow but steady decrease of both the number of clumps and gas mass fraction enclosed. The evolution of the number of clumps and masses of the high gas fraction case are therefore not influenced by the interaction as we can see by comparing the isolated (iso) and the interacting cases (dd1). In particular, no change is observed at the first pericentre passage.

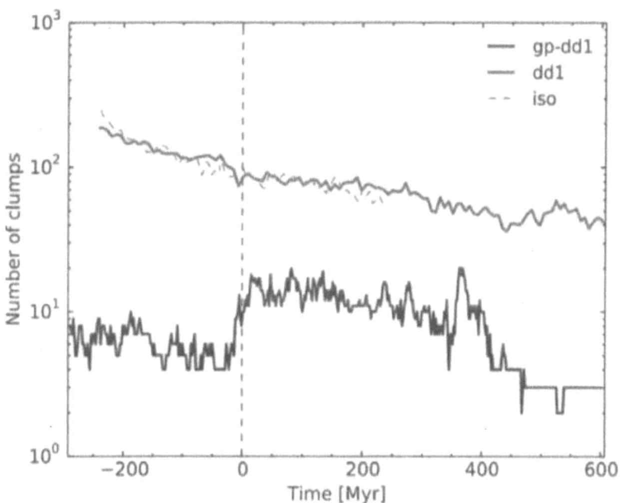

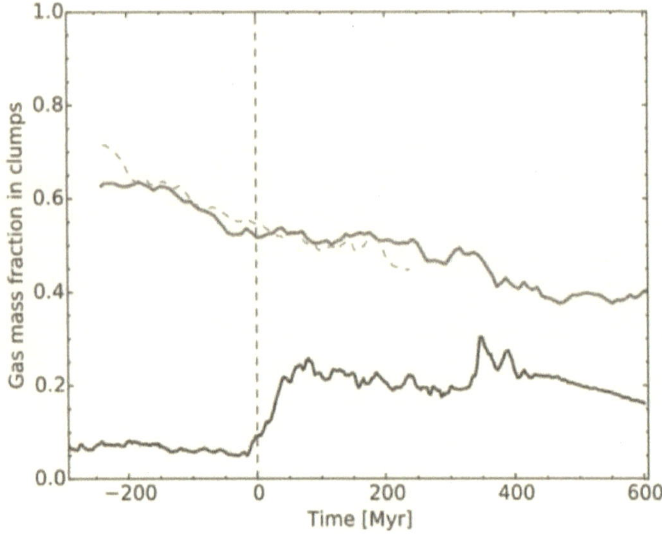

Top: number of detected clumps for the low (blue) and high (red) gas fraction for dd1 and gp-dd1. The isolated run for the high gas fraction case is also shown in dashed green. To ease the comparison, this number is multiplied by 2 for the isolated case. Bottom: gas mass fraction in gas clumps.

Evolution of the density

In the low gas fraction, this interaction-induced clumpiness condensates the gas in localized over densities. To quantify its effect on the gas density distribution, we look at the evolution of the mass-weighted density probability density function. In Fig., we see the evolution of the shape of the gas for both the low and high gas fraction cases. In the low gas fraction case, the extends to higher densities during the interaction. We also see that the of the high gas fraction case remains almost identical during the interaction and does not significantly vary from the shape of the isolated galaxy, except at the coalescence (t = 376 Myr) where there is an increase of the mass with densities above 3 × 104 cm−3.

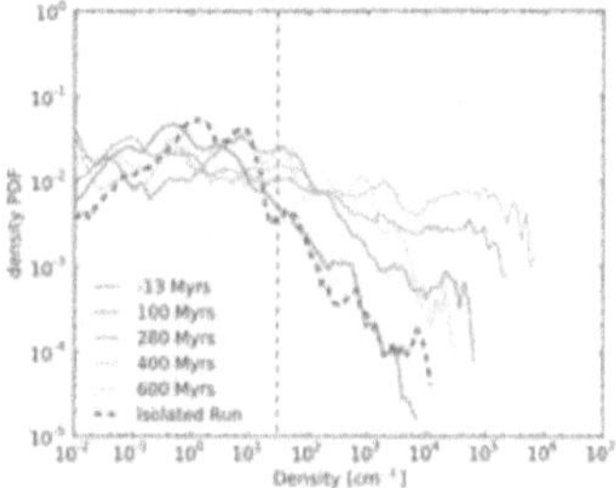

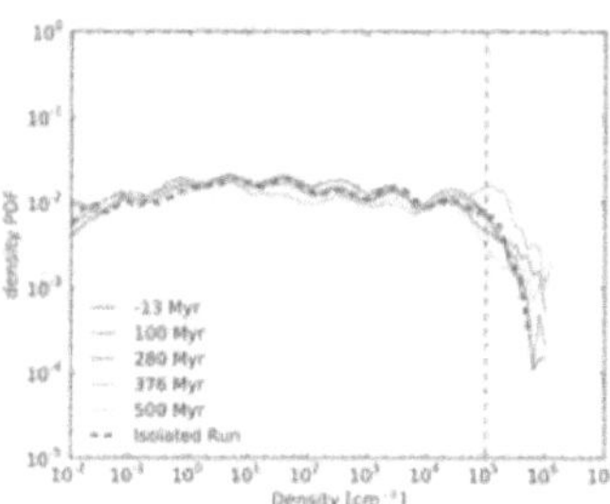

Normalized mass-weighted probability distribution function of the gas density, at several epochs (t = 0 corresponds to the first pericentre). These times correspond to before the first pericentre, shortly after the first pericentre, before the coalescence, peak of SFR during coalescence, long after the coalescence, respectively. Curves are shown for the direct–direct encounter on orbit #1 for the low (left) and high (right) gas fraction cases in solid lines. The thick purple lines show the corresponding isolated cases. The black dashed line indicates the density threshold for star formation as defined.

The evolution of the shape of the PDF is of particular interest, as high-density gas fuels star formation. Indeed, in the low gas fraction case, the gas mass above the density threshold goes from 4 to 20 per cent after the first pericentre passage and 40 per cent at the coalescence, while it stays constant, at 2–3 per cent, in the high gas fraction case.

Merger-induced star formation

Star formation histories

The comparison between low and high gas fraction star formation histories during the interaction is shown in Fig. 5. In the low gas fraction case, the SFR is about 1–2 M⊙ yr−1 before the interaction and increases to ~30 M⊙ yr−1 and more than 50 M⊙ yr−1 after the first pericentre passage. The SFR then lowers back to a few M⊙ yr−1 before increasing again to ~40–60 M⊙ yr−1 during the final coalescence.

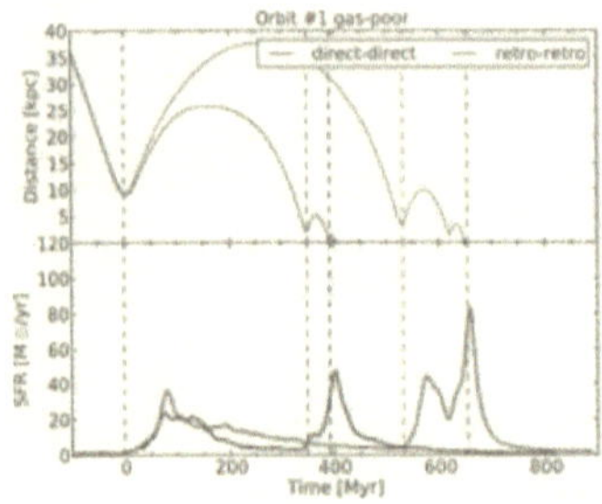

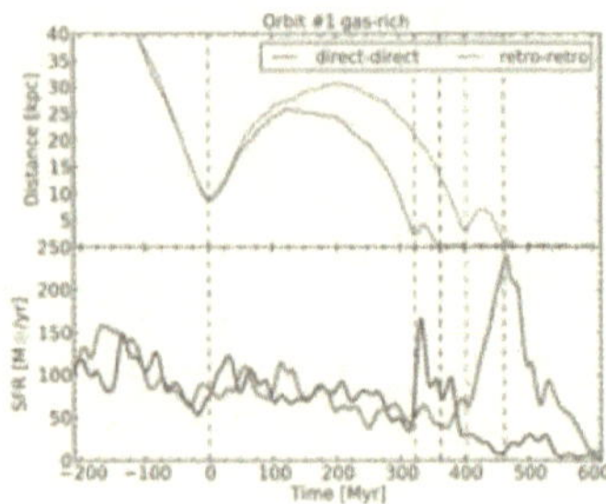

SFR during the simulations run on orbit #1, with the distance between the galaxies plotted above. The direct–direct and retro–retro simulations are shown, respectively, in blue and red. The low gas fraction case is shown on the left-hand panel and the high gas fraction case on the right-hand panel. The dashed lines correspond to the time of the first pericentre passage (in black) and the respective times of second pericentre passage and coalescence (in the colour corresponding to the simulation).

The high gas fraction case shows a very different history. The SFR is initially relatively high, ≃120 M⊙ yr−1 for the galaxy pair, and does not increase significantly at the first pericentre passage. The SFR is only enhanced at the coalescence,4 and only by a factor at most 5. Increasing only the gas fraction thus appears to significantly lower the boost of SFR.

To ensure that this results does not depend on a particularity of the chosen orbit or orientation, we also look at the SFR of the two other tested orbits and orientations, which are displayed in Fig. . We see that they follow the behaviour of orbit #1; they all show almost no increase of star formation at the first pericentre passage, and a mild burst at coalescence.

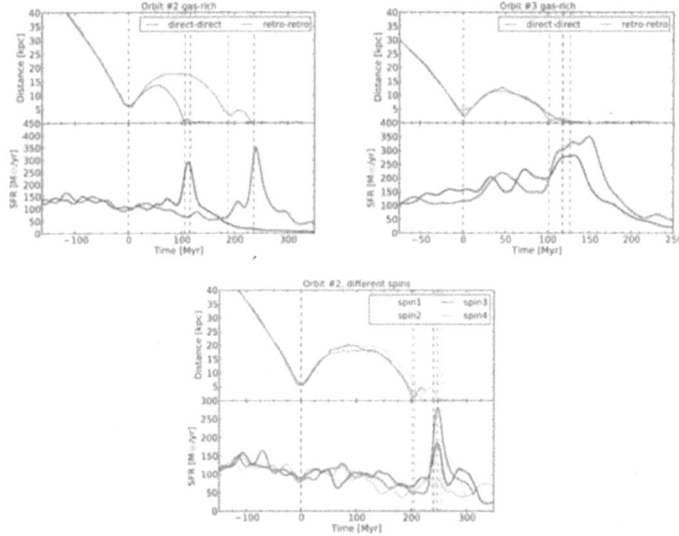

The starburst sequence

Our motivation to run these simulations resides in the fact that a smaller than expected number of high-redshift galaxies are found on the starburst sequence of both the M⋆–SFR and Σgas–ΣSFR diagrams, the latter being also known as the Schmidt–Kennicutt diagram.

In Fig., we can see the evolution of our simulated galaxies on the Schmidt–Kennicutt diagram. The computation is done in a box of 60 kpc×60 kpc×60 kpc and we rescale the curves so that the pre-merger discs lie on the disc sequence. To better quantify the starbursting behaviour of our simulations, we define the starburstiness parameter as the measured ΣSFR over the value of

ΣSFR corresponding to the disc sequence of Genzel et al. (2010) for the measured Σgas. We define starbursting galaxies as galaxies with a starburstiness exeeding 4, meaning that they stand more than 0.6 dex above the disc sequence, which is a common definition for the starburst sequence.

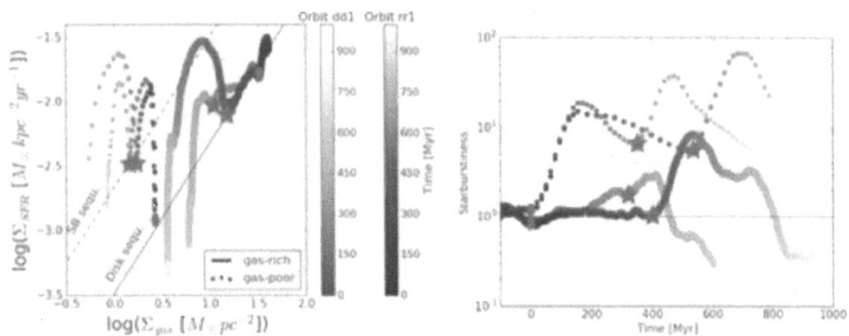

Evolution of the simulations dd1 (shades of blue) and rr1 (shades of red) on the Schmidt–Kennicutt diagram. The solid lines show the high gas fraction cases, and the dotted lines the low gas fraction cases. The red dots and stars show, respectively, the time of the first and second pericentres. The solid and dashed black lines are, respectively, the disc and starburst sequences from Genzel et al. (2010). The curve is smoothed using a constant kernel on the previous 100 Myr, to resemble the smoothing of the measurements of the SFR using IR luminosity. Bottom panel: evolution of the starburstiness, as defined in the text, during the interaction. The colours and labels are the same as in the upper panel. The black solid line indicates a starburstiness of unity, i.e. an SFR equivalent to the disc sequence for a given, Σgas, and the dotted line shows a starburstiness of 4, which we define as the lower limit to be considered as a starburst galaxy.

We see that the galaxies follow the disc sequence until the collision which shifts their loci towards the starburst sequence. The low gas fraction systems reach the starburst sequence already at the first pericentre passage and their starburstiness stays above

4 all along the starburst, that is for more than 700 Myr for the considered orbit. The high gas fraction pairs hardly reach the starburst sequence: the gas-rich direct–direct starburstiness always stays below 4 and is thus never considered as a starburst galaxy. The burst at the coalescence of the gas-rich retrograde–retrograde encounter makes it reach the starburst sequence of the Schmidt–Kennicutt diagram, but only for ~100 Myr.

In the following, we analyse the processes that influence the ability of high fraction gas merger to trigger starbursts, as compared to low gas fraction ones.

WHAT CAUSES THIS WEAK ENHANCEMENT OF STAR FORMATION?

Weak increase of the central gas inflows

Observed starbursting galaxies show a prominent nuclear starburst, with an important concentration of gas in the central kpc of the galaxies. Fig. 8 shows the fraction of SFR located in the central kpc of the galaxies. We see that at the coalescence, the peak of star formation is almost entirely located in this central kpc.5

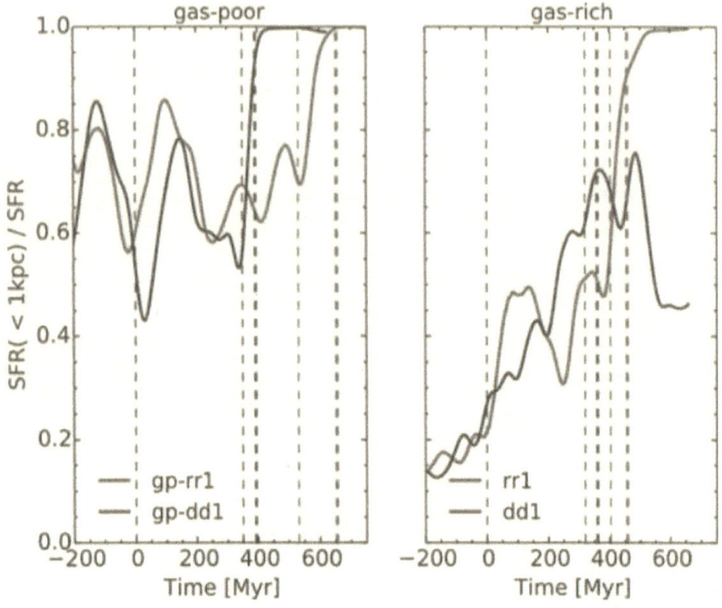

Evolution of the fraction of SFR located inside the central kpc of both galaxies for the encounters on orbit #1 in the low gas fraction case (left) and high gas fraction cases (right).

This centrally concentrated star formation is fuelled by gas inflows towards the centre. Interaction-driven gravitational torques are indeed expected to drive a large amount of gas towards the nuclei of both galaxie. In Fig., we show the inflows of baryonic mass in the central kpc of our galaxies. For the low gas fraction case, pre-merger discs have central mass inflows of $\simeq$2–3 M⊙ yr−1. Between the first and second pericentre, the discs are perturbed and the inflows have a higher mean value of about 20 M⊙ yr−1, with some important variation over time. At coalescence, the inflows reach a peak at 20 M⊙ yr−1 for the dd1 and 50 M⊙ yr−1 for the rr1 simulation, which are both at least 10 times higher than the initial gas inflows in the isolated case.

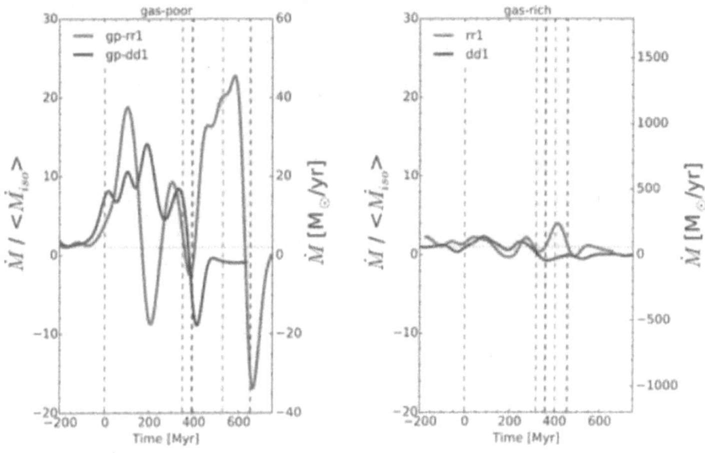

Evolution of the inflow of baryonic mass fraction in the central kpc of both galaxies for the encounters on orbit #1 in the low gas fraction case (left) and high gas fraction case (right). The left axis shows the ratio of the inflow to the mean inflow rate of the isolated run, and the same scale is used for both plots to emphasize the relative difference to the isolated case. The right axis shows the actual value of the inflow rate. The curves are smoothed using a Gaussian kernel of root-mean-square width 30 Myr for the sake of clarity.

For the high gas fraction case, the central inflows are stronger from the beginning, ≃30–50 M⊙ yr−1. As in the low gas fraction case, a strong peak in inflows is seen for the rr1 simulation, at 250 M⊙ yr−1. The relative increase compared to the pre-merger case is less than 5, much less than for the low gas fraction case. The resulting increase in SFR is also comparatively less important than for the low gas fraction case.

Central gas inflows are already strong in the pre-merger high gas fraction disc because of the VDI; the high turbulence of the gas is in part fuelled inwards by the migration of gas. Another physical explanation for the higher increase of the central inflows in low gas fraction discs is the presence of a more massive stellar component which creates a tidally induced bar or spiral arms which exert strong torques on the gas, and which adds to the effect of the gravitational torques originating from the companion. The stellar component being less populated in the high gas fraction case, this process is less efficient, as already noted by Hopkins et al. (2009).

The high gas fraction, which leads to a high turbulence and the formation of clumps, also drives strong gas inflows in the isolated discs. As a result, interaction-induced gas inflows are less important with respect to pre-merger inflows for high gas fraction discs than for low gas fraction discs. This leads to a lower increase of SFR due to central gas inflows.

Mild enhancement of gas turbulence

Our current understanding of extended starburst in low gas fraction galaxy interactions is that the increase of the SFR is caused by an increase of gas turbulence.

We compute the one-dimensional velocity dispersion of the gas, along the line of sight of the simulations at the scale of 100 pc and plot its evolution in Fig. We see that the pre-interaction velocity dispersion is much higher in the high gas fraction case, $\sigma \simeq$ 35 km s−1, than in the low gas fraction case, $\sigma \simeq$ 10 km s−1. This agrees with observations and is due to the gas phase which is more gravitationally unstable with high gas fraction. The interaction brings the velocity dispersion of the low gas fraction case to more than 40 km s−1, in agreement with both observations and previous simulations. In the high gas fraction case, the velocity dispersion goes up to around 60 km s−1 only. The relative increase in turbulence is much higher in the low gas fraction case, a factor of 5, to be compared to the high gas fraction case, which shows an increase of less than a factor of 2.

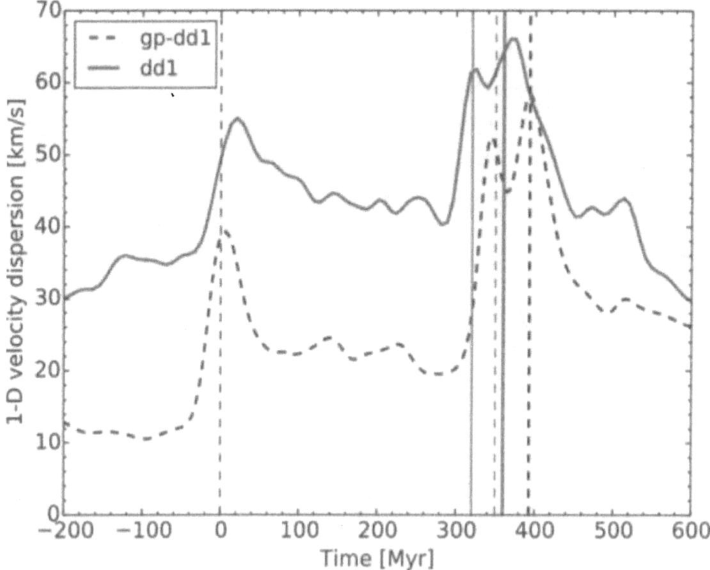

Evolution of the gas velocity dispersion of the direct–direct simulations on orbit #1. The low gas fraction is depicted by the blue dashed curve and the high gas fraction by the solid red line.

If we suppose, for convenience, that the gravitational specific energy is equally transferred between the gas, stars, and DM during the interaction, we can write, for a time-scale much shorter than that of the dissipation of the turbulence at the scale of clumps (i.e. $\ll$10 Myr):

$$\frac{3}{2} M_{\mathrm{gas}} \sigma_{\mathrm{f}}^2 = \frac{3}{2} M_{\mathrm{gas}} \sigma_{\mathrm{i}}^2 + M_{\mathrm{gas}} f \Delta \phi,$$

where σi and σf are the initial and final one-dimensional velocity dispersions, Δϕ is the difference in gravitational potential, and f is the fraction of this potential energy which is transferred to the turbulent motion during the interaction, and which we suppose to be a constant. After the above assumptions, Mgas disappears on both sides of the equation, which therefore applies for both gas fraction regimes. It follows that, for the same fΔϕ:

$$\sigma_{\mathrm{f}} = \sqrt{\sigma_i^2 + \frac{2}{3} f \Delta\phi}$$

for both the low and high gas fraction case. Hence, if fΔϕ brings σ from 10 to 40 km s−1 in the low gas fraction case, it will increase σ from 40 to ≃55 km s−1 in the high gas fraction case, which is approximately what we measure in our simulations. It is interesting to note that the required value of fΔϕ to increase σ from 10 to 40 km s−1 in our calculation happens to be less than the specific gravitational energy liberated in 10 Myr (time-scale for dissipation of turbulence) for the masses considered here, when the distance between the two galaxies is smaller than 25 kpc, i.e. ~50 Myr before the first pericentre for orbit #1. This is the correct order of magnitude for the onset of the rise of the velocity dispersion in our simulations.

This heuristic calculation shows the difficulty of increasing the velocity dispersion while it is already high, which leads to a mild increase in gas turbulence from interactions in high gas fraction discs.

Absence of interaction-induced tidal compression

The increase in compressive turbulence is thought to be driven by the onset of fully compressive tides. On top of triggering compressive turbulence, fully compressive tides also reduce the Jeans mass and help gas fragmentation in star-forming clumps (Jog 2013, 2014). Extended regions undergoing fully compressive tides are a common feature of galaxy encounters.

To measure the impact of compressive tides on our galaxies, we compute the tidal tensor defined by its components Tij = −∂i∂jϕ using first-order finite differences of the total gravitational force at the scale of 50 pc. The tidal field is compressive if the maximum eigenvalue of the tensor is negative. The method is the same as R14. Results for the low and high gas fraction runs on the Orbit #1 are shown on Fig. .

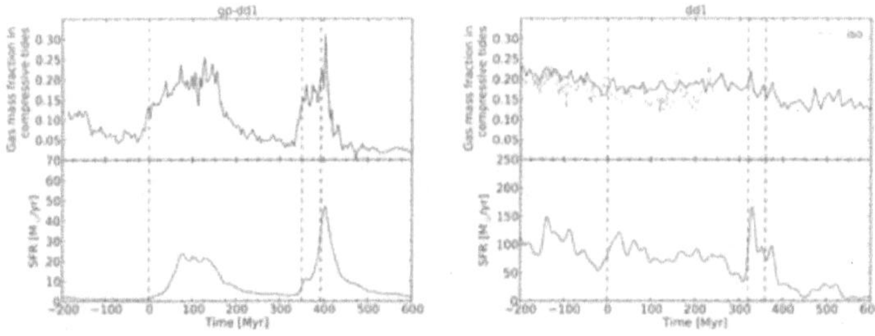

Evolution of the gas mass fraction in a fully compressive tidal field (top panel) compared to the SFR (bottom panel) for the direct–direct encounter on orbit #1 in the low gas fraction case (left) and high gas fraction case (right).

We see that, in the low gas fraction case, the gas mass fraction in compressive tides increases from 7 to 20 per cent during the pericentre passages. These values are similar to those obtained in previous simulations of galaxy interactions.

In the high gas fraction case, the mass gas fraction in compressive tides is initially higher and tend to slowly and monotically decrease with time, with no significant changes induced by the pericentre passages.

This high but steady gas mass fraction in compressive tides results from the matter distribution of the galaxy. In Fig. , we show the position of tidally compressive regions $\simeq$60 Myr after the first pericentre passage. In the low gas fraction case, we see that tidally compressive regions develop over extended regions close to the galaxy nuclei, in the forming tidal tails and in the bridges between the two galaxies. In the high gas fraction case, the tidally compressive regions are mainly located inside the clumps. The gravitational potential is locally dominated by the highly concentrated clumps, leaving the interclump medium in tidally extensive zones which makes the formation of any zone of compressive tides harder, and limits any increase in gas fragmentation during the interaction.

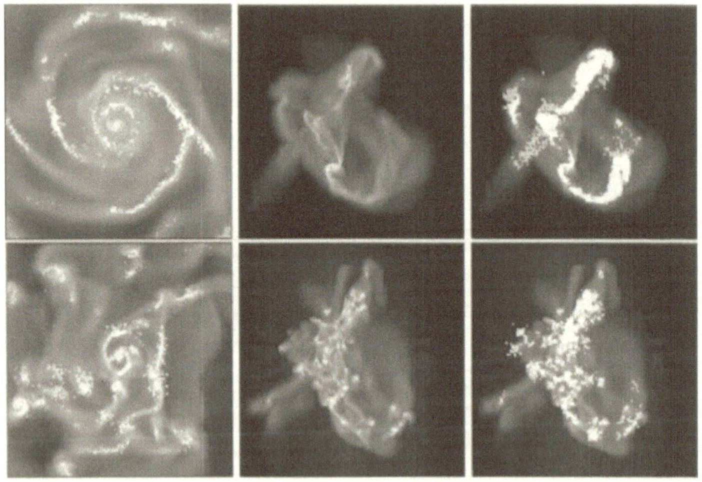

Gas density maps for the gas-poor (top panel) and gas-rich (bottom panel) simulations. The left-hand panels show the isolated galaxies. The central and right-hand panels show the direct–direct interaction for orbit #1 at t = 60 Myr. The maps span 10 kpc × 10 kpc for the isolated runs and 50 kpc × 50 kpc for the merger runs.

This adds to the small enhancement of the turbulence, which limits an increase in compressive turbulence, and thus a change in the density PDF and in the interaction-induced SFR.

In summary, our numerical simulations show that the clumpy nature driven by the high gas fraction has a strong influence on the central inflows, the gas turbulence and the compressive tides. These three physical processes are seen to be enhanced during low-redshift encounters and are thought to be responsible for the interaction-driven starburst in low-redshift galaxies. In the high gas fraction cases, these three processes are already strong in isolated galaxies and are not further enhanced by interactions.

Our simulations hereby confirm the importance of these three processes in the increase of the SFR in gas-poor interactions and we claim that their weak enhancement for high gas fraction discs explains the relative diminished efficiency of gas-rich major mergers to trigger starbursts.

No effect of saturation from feedback

The SFR of the high gas fraction discs in isolation is $\simeq$60 times higher than that for the low gas fraction discs, the net feedback energy from SNe explosions and H II regions is therefore also much higher. One can wonder whether an increase of star formation is not self-regulated in high gas fraction discs because of the stellar feedback.

To test this hypothesis, we restart the dd1 simulations, but with all sources of feedback, which were presented, turned off. One should note that an absence of feedback for a long period of time would transform significantly the structure of the galaxies, as stellar feedback regulates the growth of gas clumps. Shutting off feedback just before the investigated event, i.e. the galactic encounters, ensures that we compare galaxies with the most similar structure as possible. Therefore, we shut off the feedback around 40 Myr only before the two moments when a rise of SFR is expected, namely the first pericentre passage and the coalescence. The time-scale of dissipation of the turbulence being around 10 Myr (Mac Low 1999) at the clumps scale, which is comparable to the free-fall time, we ensure that there is no more influence of the feedback on the gas turbulence at the expected starburst time.

The evolution of the SFR for the feedback case and no-feedback case is plotted in Fig. . We see that there is a small increase in SFR, especially at coalescence, in the simulations without feedback, but the general behaviour does not change; even without stellar feedback, the interaction only induces a small starburst compared to the low gas fraction case.

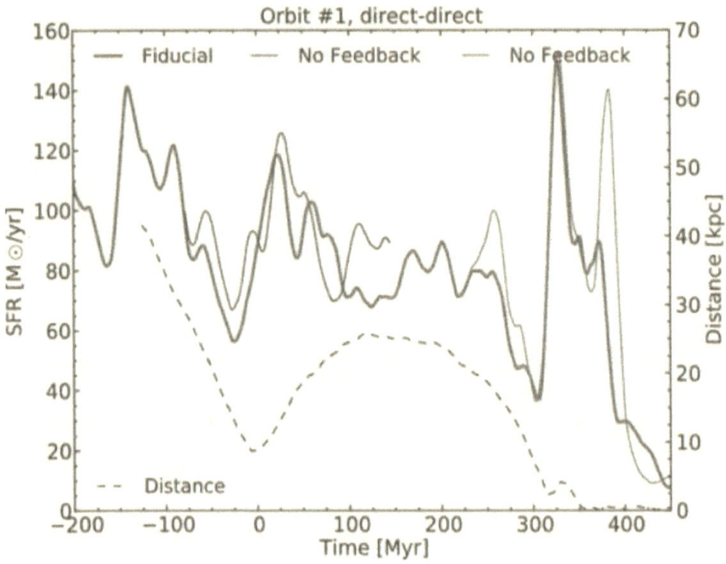

Evolution of the SFR for the dd1 simulation and runs with turned off stellar feedback at different times. The red solid line shows the SFR of the fiducial run, dd1, presented in Fig. . The blue and green lines show the SFR resulting from the runs without feedback. They separate from the fiducial curve slightly before the time delay indicated in the text because of the curve smoothing. The black dashed line shows the distance between the two galaxies.

Our simulations show that our feedback implementation, which allows a burst of star formation for low gas fraction major mergers, is not responsible for the weakness of the star formation enhancement in the high gas fraction case. The implementation of subgrid models of stellar feedback in numerical simulations is a long-standing issue. Energy outputs from SNe and stellar winds are theoretically rather well understood for most stellar populations (see the review by Dale 2015), but the details in the numerical implementations are important and can lead to significantly different results. A detailed study of the impact of the implementation of feedback on galaxy structure is beyond the scope of this paper.

On the one hand, our no-feedback simulations show that a weaker feedback than ours would not produce a strong enhancement of star formation either. On the other hand, a stronger feedback would increase the pre-interaction overall gas turbulence. As we have seen, the interaction-induced increase of turbulence would be even smaller which would lead to an even weaker enhancement of the SFR. This shows that the weakness of merger-driven starbursts at high redshift (compared to low-redshift cases) does not result from saturation by feedback in our models, and this result could only be stronger if real feedback had more important effects in high-redshift galaxies.

www.ingramcontent.com/pod-product-compliance
Lightning Source LLC
LaVergne TN
LVHW041059150826
845673LV00007B/1846

* 9 7 9 8 8 9 2 7 7 4 3 5 2 *